To
My brother in Chr...
Don't settle for
the normal.

RoD.
GTL
3-11-22

# Me
# Jesus
# a Beer
# and
# a Cigar

# Me
# Jesus
# a Beer
# and
# a Cigar

———∝———

By

## Bob Dickinson

XULON PRESS

Xulon Press
2301 Lucien Way #415
Maitland, FL 32751
407.339.4217
www.xulonpress.com

Paperback ISBN-13: 978-1-6628-3853-8
Hard Cover ISBN-13: 978-1-6628-3854-5
eBook ISBN-13: 978-1-6628-3855-2

# What's in a Name... or a Title?

**Perhaps you picked up this book because of the title. Uh,** oh. Didn't anyone ever tell you not to judge a book by its cover? But hey, if it worked in this case, great. Much appreciated.

Ever wonder how titles are chosen? In many cases, the publisher chooses. Oh sure, the author almost always begins with a preconceived title and cover, but the publisher says, "Not so fast." It edits. Rearranges. It changes this. It changes that. And all of a sudden *All's Well That Ends Well* becomes *War and Peace* and *Atticus* becomes *To Kill a Mockingbird*.

I was pretty insistent about the title of this book, however. It had to be *Me, Jesus, a Beer, and a Cigar*. Because that was the inspiration. And as we all know, writers must be inspired. Yeah, we all believe that crock.

But in my case, it was true. Of course.

At the end of most weeks, I shut down early. I shut down to take a look back on my week. And reflect. Not just my week. But my life.

There is a micro-brewery in this little town outside of Atlanta where I live. Every Friday afternoon, weather permitting, I wander to that micro-brew's back deck. For some reason, it is normally uninhabited. Not sure why. But it is. Occasionally, someone lights upon another part of the deck. It is a big deck. Sometimes we smile. Express cordialities. Even talk. Cass is a talker. But that's a story for another time. I soon learned everyone was there for a reason.

With beer in hand, I'd light a cigar. Usually a Rocky Patel. Or an Evo. I slide back comfortably into my Adirondack chair. Baseball cap.

Sunglasses. Music being piped through the speakers hung on the massive tree centered in the deck. Dan Fogelberg. Journey. Credence Clearwater Revival. Green Day. James Taylor. Van Morrison. Cheryl Crow. Boys to Men. Others.

And there...I sit. And think. And reflect. And listen. And learn.

No matter how good or bad the week had been, I come away enlightened. Often with an action plan. Feeling better. Yeah, the beer and cigar may have had some influence there.

Sometimes the plan is to lean in. At other times, just shut up and listen. Allow for time to play out its course.

I learned I was not in control. And became okay with that.

# Not a Foreword

**I don't think I want a "Foreword" in this book. I always** wondered why books had one. Perhaps it was because it was in the Foreword part of the book. But that's improper English. And we never do that. Never veer from the structure of the King's English. Always follow subject, verb, object of verb. Of course, with proper punctuation. Tongue in cheek.

How boring. Many great writers—of which I am not—have chosen to throw "proper English" aside for their own style. E.E. Cummings was oft averse to capitalization. William Faulkner was the master of the run-on sentence. They're both thought of pretty highly. Style is important. It defines your writing. It can even define you. So. As you will notice along the way, I don't necessarily conform... to that which my English teachers espoused while attempting to educate me.

I actually think they really did a pretty good job, though. I majored in English. Although it wasn't because I was in love with Shakespeare or Balzac. It was because I loved to write. Once I realized that I was not going to be a professional baseball player, I thought I might try my hand at writing. Novelist. Yeah. That would be perfect. Well, let's recategorize that to "best-selling" novelist. Otherwise, I'd starve. My confidence wasn't up to that.

So, I told myself that because I loved sports and loved to write, I would become a sports writer. I had an offer right out of college to come to Daytona Beach to join the News-Journal sports department. I knew I'd get all the crap assignments. But I knew that's what starting at the bottom meant. I was okay with that. What wasn't okay was the salary - $5,400. A year. Now, admittedly this was a much earlier era, but when I ran the figures on my every-two-week after taxes paycheck, it came to about $165. Or $360 a month. Gulp.

There had to be another option. And there was. Sports public relations. That's how I started. Jumped right into professional football right out of college. An NFL team did its preseason training on my college campus during the summer, and one summer I stayed for summer school. I told my parents the reason was to get ahead on my classes so I would have extra time to look for a job the spring before graduation. But the real reason was to hang around that team and its PR execs. Pete Rozelle was the PR king for the Los Angeles Rams before being named NFL Commissioner. That's what I wanted to be. NFL Commissioner. One day.

But no. My first professional team was not an NFL team. It was with the "Wiffle." WFL. World Football League. The job lasted only four months and then blew up as the league ran out of cash. I was handed a check in the middle of the week (which I knew was a bad sign) and told to go downstairs to the bank immediately and cash it before the players were given theirs at the end of practice that day. Many of theirs would be worthless.

At least I formed a great relationship with my boss with whom I would go on to work several times over the next couple of decades. Not all lost.

But I digress.

Me, Jesus, a Beer, and a Cigar is about being a bit unorthodox. I was raised in a great Christian home and witnessed one of the greatest love stories I could have ever imagined between my mom and dad. I "came to the Lord" when I was 11, the seed planted at a Billy Graham Crusade at Philadelphia's Franklin Field.

I became a youth leader in the church, a leader at school complete with great grades and all-star abilities in sports. I married my college sweetheart. Then divorced her six years later.

I was mess. Even though, I thought I was okay - so long as my career seemed headed in the right direction. Through the years, I've come to understand that God can get you through all those messes.

Even when you're moments away from swerving your car into the front of a barreling 18-wheeler only inches from the other side of the white line.

I had a friend once who insistently kept telling me, "Everything is going to be okay." Maybe that friend was the voice of God whether they realized it or not.

Yes, my life was a bit unorthodox. Faith-driven highs followed by immense failures. Or at least I imagined them to be immense. Truth is. Everyone has failures. How we respond to them tells us everything we need to know about ourselves. Failures are how God grows us.

I don't feel that I look at life through normal lenses. There is nothing normal about life. You know how I know that? Because if you asked a million people what was "normal," you would get a million answers. Although for some reason, we all seek "normal." We shouldn't. We should seek the abnormal. We should strive to be abnormal.

The world doesn't experience necessary change through normalcy. One of my favorite expressions is "if nothing changes, then nothing ever changes." Think about it. I don't know who coined that. Maybe I'll take credit.

The way I view Christ and God is not normal either. And it shouldn't be normal for anyone. Whatever normal is. (See earlier paragraph). Because a relationship with the Creator is a one-on-one relationship. He made you distinct. There is no one else like you. Therefore, your normal or abnormal life is unlike anyone else's. And only God knows what you will achieve and how you will relate to Him.

Look, we have all been given completely unique gifts and talents. Those that are ours alone. We need to figure out how to use them the way God intended. Try to steer down a different road, and it likely won't be pretty. That's sometimes where the failure occurs. We may resist. People may not understand us or look at us strangely if our talents take us down an abnormal road. There's that concept again. Normal. Abnormal.

Theology is not normal either. Every denomination thinks they have a corner or inside track on what God wants them to believe, study and how to live. There are many parallels. But also varying "twists."

Some believe you have to be dunked for salvation. Others believe you get lucky and are predestined to go to heaven even before birth. And still others believe that you can't have a one-on-one relationship with Christ because you have to go through some sort of intermediary.

I have a friend who once had the extraordinary experience of leading a Grand Iman to Christ. It was the first person he ever brought to the Lord. It was on a bench in a deep, dark corner of a park continents away. He actually thought he was going to be killed. Instead, the first question the Iman asked about my friend's Christianity was, "so why do you have so many denominations?"

"Gee, I don't know," was his answer. "I'm just a follower of Christ and his teachings and know that he has changed me and my heart."

I think the Christian church gets its panties in a wad too much over denominations and theology. Give me a good, mixed-culture non-denominational church, and I'll show you some movement for God's kingdom...the one that says love thy neighbor as thyself. And love God.

So, it shouldn't surprise you that *Me, Jesus, a Beer, and a Cigar* is a bit edgy at times. One thing I've discovered over the years is that if you are comfortable, you are not working or doing enough to make this world a better place. I hesitate to say "further His kingdom" because I think there are far too many Christians who have a distorted view of what the kingdom should look like—namely like them.

Lean in. Become uncomfortable.

# Part Two

My writings began a few weeks before the killing of George Floyd. COVID-19 had slowed my small business immeasurably. Confusion. What information do I believe about the virus? What happens next? How long?

Unrest. People were upset. Then George Floyd. People took to the streets. Frustration was rampant. Many didn't even know why. They just knew that things were really messed up socially, economically, racially, spiritually, politically, physically, healthily. They wrapped their arms around one or a couple of those abnormalities and began to take a stance. Some worthy. Some not. Some succumbed to deeper trauma.

The presidential election was hitting full stride. It was not pretty. Time to hit the pause button. So, I did.

I did not panic. I knew a door was opening. Perhaps at least a window.

Ever notice how when life gets really crazy and begins to go askew, people begin to work extra hard, long, and frantically trying to find some way to fix things that aren't...well...normal to them? I used to be like that. I remember once working a 116-hour week. I remember working for six straight months without taking a day off. To find answers. All to get to the mountaintop.

It didn't work.

It was the pandemic spring. But it didn't seem like spring. No meeting friends at an outside café. Or for a beer. Or for a cigar. Or to talk about life. Or God. Or not. No baseball. No nothin'.

My alarm went off at its usual time, 4:15 a.m. Mornings are my quiet time. I have a regular routine of motivational readings. Paul Tripp. Sarah Evans. This guy called Jesus. But this day, I pushed the pause button.

I had one simple question. What next?

The one thing I've learned over the years is that when life is getting to be too much, I am doing too much. I now forcefully withdraw into a period of quiet where I do one thing and one thing only.

Listen.

So that morning I listened. I learned God had given me talents and gifts for a reason. And that mine were unlike anyone else's. Sometimes we choose to go against the grain of those God-given gifts and talents because we simply want to. Or we see an enticing direction we want to go and don't really give much thought as to whether we are using our talents. We just want "it." Whatever "it" is.

That morning I heard: *"The world is upside down right now because it needs to be upside down. In order to learn some things about itself. About others. About things being ignored. I am still in control. And will always be in control. But this is a teaching moment."*

So, what was I to learn during this teaching moment?

*"Stop doing what you are doing. Look around you. You see people in need. How are you going to help them?"*

I don't know. That's a big ask.

*"Take the talents and heart that I've given you - and reach out. Don't worry about your business. From now on, I'm in charge of that. Look to those in need. Look to circumstances that need righting. Lean on relationships that I put in front of you. Get involved. Whether it's comfortable for you or not.*

*"I'll help."*

Really? Well. Ok then.

Within the next several weeks, I marched for racial and social injustice, publicly challenged the status quo of a professional sports team's name that was denigrating and began writing weekly. Thoughts for everyday living were gaining momentum...

# Table of Contents

# Contents

# More Not a Foreword

**Writing a book is not easy. Organizing it is even more** difficult. My first idea was simply to write an introduction and a conclusion then insert each new "thought for everyday living" in the order in which I wrote them and say, "Ta-da!"

As I floated the idea, it went nowhere. B-O-R-I-N-G!

Through a chance meeting, an acquaintance turned into new friend. She lived in Dallas. She had completed her first book. I asked how she found the publisher. She said it was not easy but provided a few tips. First one was pray. Yeah. Should have thought of that one.

"Lord, give me something so big that it is doomed to fail lest you be in it."

That was a start.

I continued to put my epiphanies in order as I wrote them. No. Too easy. What about by alphabetical order of title? No. Too trite. What about grouping them by themes. Not bad. But I began to feel like I was throwing all of them into a box, shaking them up, and rearranging them just in a different order.

Hmmm. Good point. I needed something else.

What if I provided comments after every one explaining and giving context to what influenced me to write that particular entry? Perhaps a memory. A happy spot. A sad moment. A current event. A crossroad. A tragedy. A miracle. What are some of the between-the-line messages? The symbolism. Metaphors.

I like it. That's good. Let's do that.

So. What next? This was beginning to look a bit like a roller coaster. Yeah. That's it. A roller coaster.

Today's world may often seem like a roller coaster. We're all riding it. Sharp curves. Ups. Downs. Steep hills. Fast descents. More sharp curves and jolting starts and stops.

*Me, Jesus, a Beer, and a Cigar* intends to stimulate thinking. We all think—every minute of the day. Those thoughts may be reflective, automatic, intuitive, self-critical, hopeful, frightening or just plain... normal, or at least what we perceive to be normal.

There is nothing normal about daily living, though. Think about what was normal three weeks ago. Six weeks ago. Six months ago. A year ago. So much has changed.

I don't profess to be clairvoyant or an expert. But what I do believe is that people need to inspect their lives continually. And think. Think productive thoughts. So, I will foster, stimulate, and encourage just that. On a wide variety of topics: politics, religion, sports, entertainment, society, business, and science just to name a few.

My guess is you may wonder what proclivities I have regarding the variety of topics just mentioned. For that you'll have to wait and see. What!? You think I will tip my hand immediately? Actually, the better answer is, I may not be sure what those tendencies, inclinations and predispositions actually are.

I like to think of myself as a Larry King-style host, simply asking questions and presenting situations—perhaps weighing in—but more to get you thinking thoughts about how you really feel about the topic. Admittedly, some writings will leave you feeling really good and inspired. Others may simply piss you off. Constantly, I will encourage and challenge you to reach out and really make a difference out there.

That is the intent. Society is incredibly diverse. And I encourage you, the reader, to not fall back instinctively on your unconscious prejudices and biases, but to try to see various points of view. In the end, you may say you've tried but you weren't moved. Then again, I hope there are scenarios you can admit you've never thought of in that way or from that point of view.

# Part Two

I will admit. Even though I knew I had a lot to say, I didn't really know how this was going to turn out or where I was going to dig up topics, stories and thoughts.

I also didn't want to browbeat people with my own opinions. Gosh, that's exactly what was going awry in society. So, the question became, how can I become a storyteller with underlying messages that convey what God wants me to share without becoming overtly heavy-handed with that God-thing or with my personal opinion.

One driving impetus for the entries was the disparity I was seeing between politics and religion, particularly in my view, Christianity. This all came unglued in a very long column that I published a month before the 2020 presidential election. You can find that column published on a site that I contribute to periodically—"Like the Dew, A Progressive Journal of Southern Culture and Politics.'"

A lot of my Christians friends didn't agree or appreciate the stance I took. Others, gave a high five.

Unorthodox. Uncomfortable.

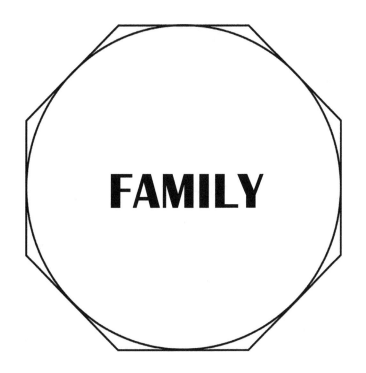

# FAMILY

# Love Story

**A father gives away his one and only daughter on her** wedding day. He has thought about this moment from the first time he laid eyes on her. But now it's here.

Where have the years gone? What can he share with her as she and her husband become one and begin a lifetime together? There is so much battering the corners of his brain. So much he feels he needs to share.

Perhaps he should share a love story—one he had the privilege to witness through his youth, the one he calls the greatest love story he could ever imagine here on earth—his parents.

Things were not always perfect. They didn't have a lot. His dad worked as a welder, a handyman, a part-time farmer. His mom was a mom - teaching and caring for him and his sister... taking them to church. It wasn't until he got older that he realized how difficult it must have been for them at times. Yet they always made it work. They always worked it out. They always gave and gave and gave, and never asked for anything in return. Over time it became a love easy to reciprocate.

He saw that in a marriage it's the little things, the simple things, that count. Mom loved roses. So, when Dad built his shop behind their little brick ranch house, unbeknownst to mom, he one day planted a whole row of rose bushes lining the shop's side that faced the house, so that every day as she washed dishes (by hand) and looked out the back kitchen window, she could see those roses.

As a part-time farmer, dad often rented fields nearby where he raised corn and wheat to sell for extra money to keep the family going. The plantings, fertilizing, cultivating and harvests were not easy for one man (and a sometimes son). He tended those fields at night after he came home from the factory and on weekends. There was no rest. He was perpetually tired. But Mom, without fail, would take a jug of water to him at some point for two reasons. First, she wanted to be sure he was okay and that he had enough water to drink on hot days. But mostly, the son believed, she just wanted to see him and spend time with him even if he was all dirty and sweaty.

So, why is this the story he needs to share?

Because, as he looks back on those days, he has come to understand that it was those little, simple things that held them together... and resulted in that incredible love story.

The wedding weekend arrives. Choking back tears, he shares the story and concludes, "As you my dear daughter and you, my new son, grow in your marriage, I encourage one to be the 'planter of roses' and the other to be the 'bearer of water.' It will make all the difference in the world."

———————⟨⟩———————

*This entry was the longest developing of any in this book. It began as the toast I wanted to deliver at my one-and-only daughter's wedding. That wedding was postponed seven months due to the pandemic and its restrictions. I kept going over again and again in my mind what I could share with her and her husband that would sink in. Resonate. Be taken to heart. Be lived.*

*What examples could I use? It could not be trite. It had to be profound. Impactful. It had to be the perfect speech for the perfect marriage. And from that came the inspiration. When I think of great marriages, I instantly think of my mom and dad. What made it such a great marriage? Why did it work so well? What did they have? What did they do that held it all together...and showed an extraordinary love?*

*I could not come up with any big "ah ha" revelation or moment or action as an example. So, I began to think of the little things. That was it! Share the little things that kept them so focused on each other. Share* the little things that showed oh so simply the great love that just kept getting better and better.

And thus, the story of the "planting of roses" and "bearer of water." For weeks going into the wedding, I rehearsed the story over and over in my head. I wrote it out. I stood in front of a mirror and practiced it. Then the night came. My palms got sweaty. My heart raced. I was going to get only one chance to share this with my daughter and her husband. I honestly don't remember a lot of how I said it. All that I know is that my daughter was in tears and that her husband gave me a huge hug. And as I looked around, a lot of people had wet eyes—even the guys. Mom and Dad must have been with me that night and hopefully smiling down ... holding hands.

# It's Beginning to Look a Lot Like Christmas

### But is it?

As a year unlike any that most of us have seen in our lifetime, did Christmas 2020 really look like other Christmases we've known through the years?

A consequence of the pandemic was that many celebrated alone. Many did not have the ability to put food on the table or gifts under the Christmas tree. Or even have a Christmas tree.

Amidst lost jobs, lost businesses, lost loved ones, Christmas 2020 for many was very empty and less than joyous.

One heartening trend was a renewed enthusiasm for looking out and helping our neighbors. "Giving Tuesday" alone that year, saw a 25 percent increase in charitable donations from $2 billion to $2.5 billion. News media continued to showcase everyday people embracing their neighbors' needs, starting campaigns and "giving" drives, reaching out to essential workers with acts of kindness.

The holiday spirit in full force, indeed.

The age-old question of who is our neighbor becomes one that many ask? The next question we should ask, though, is how well do we want to get to know that neighbor?

Is it enough to provide a box of food for the community food pantry? Is it enough to donate old or gently used clothing? Is it enough to write a sizeable check to a charitable group that is doing all the heavy lifting we wish we had time to do...but rationalize that we don't?

In many ways, the messiness of our own lives prevents us from actually connecting. Yes, our hearts are in the right place. But maybe another step needs to be taken.

A friend recently told me of a family who reached out to say they wanted to give a "family in need" a Merry Christmas. They had plenty. This year, they decided they would cut back a lot and give to a family in need that had little...that had had a tough year. Their heart was clearly in the right place.

They were surprised, however, when they heard the response.

"Yes, I can find you a family to give to. Yes, they will no doubt appreciate it. But over the years, the same thing keeps happening. People, who are faceless and often nameless, reach out at the holidays to do what they believe is kind, noble and even Christ-like.

"If you really want to make a difference in a family's life, get to know them. Intermingle with them in their world. Spend time with them. Talk to them. Learn why things are so difficult. Learn ways you can help other than simply showering gifts on them at Christmas time only to walk out of their lives and away from the real need.

"These families need more than a few gifts at Christmas. They are hurting. Learn why they are hurting and embrace them for who they are and embrace their total needs. Learn the social, economic and racial issues that may be restricting them."

The answer hit the family hard.

While a bit outside their comfort level, they understood. Isn't that what the person whom we celebrate this time of year would do?

"You're right. Set up a meeting. We'll meet them on their turf...or at least start with a Zoom call."

Next Christmas could certainly look a lot different for both families.

*This is a look back. Quite surreal and for many, Christmas 2020 was one of great fear and trepidation. One that we certainly will never forget. The masks in the holiday photos - and perhaps even Christmas cards for those attempting to smile amidst the fallout - won't let us.*

*Ten months into the worst pandemic in U.S. history, empathy was starting to rear its head. Giving was up as we looked at our neighbors and saw great need. And recognized new neighbors of different* backgrounds and circumstances for the first time. The election was over. And while divisiveness was still apparent, calm was setting in at least for the holidays as many yearned for the distraction and a time of giving.

We wanted to help. But many didn't know how. And those who thought they did, sometimes, needed simply to turn the glass a quarter turn to get a better perspective. This revelation is what the well-intended family experienced.

# Two Sons...and a Father

**They met at a coffee house. Justus had driven three** hours. Business meeting mid-day. Coffee with his brother, Atty, late afternoon. Drive back.

Atticus, his brother called him "Atty", lived there. He invited Justus to spend the night. They had not spent much time together over the last year. But Justus was in a hurry to get back. A catch-up over coffee was fine.

It was a trendy neighborhood java joint—not one of those perfunctory conglomerates. Atty arrived early and found a booth toward the rear. He'd wait until his brother arrived, then offer to buy the coffee. He checked his cellphone for texts. *Was Justus running on time? Do I need to stop on the way home to pick up anything for dinner? Was Dad doing okay?*

Their father lived nearby, but alone. He preferred it that way. Independent. Wise. Gracious. Still active in the community. In Atty's eyes, he was a great role model. Tough at times, but always loving and giving.

Justus came blowing through the coffee house door. He appeared a bit anxious, agitated to some degree. He looked around and didn't see Atty. Anxiety heightened.

Atty stood up and waved. Justus scurried to the back booth. Atty prepared to embrace his brother, but Justus quickly stuck out his hand and fell into the opposite side of the booth.

"So how are you doing?" asked Atty. He smiled. It was good to see his brother again. It had been a while.

"Ah, man, you know...ups and downs and a bunch of run-arounds," was the response.

Justus gave him an overview of the hectic drive to town. Stormy conditions. Delays. Late for his big business deal.

"Ya know, they just don't get it," he uttered. "I don't know what I have to do or say to make it clear how much they need me and our firm. Tons of data. Best sales pitch I can muster. And they are still clueless."

"That's too bad," said Atty. "What do they need? What are they trying to accomplish?"

"Hell, I don't know. I don't know that *they* know. Frustrating. We're perfect for them, but they just aren't listening."

Atty wondered whether Justus had it backward.

"Have you talked to Dad lately?" Atty asked.

"Man, there's another frustration. All he ever wants to tell me is what I'm doing wrong. I don't visit enough. I don't do this. I don't do that. What do you think about such-and-such? I tell him I'm busting my balls, but that seems to go in one ear and out the other. I don't need to be disciplined any more. I manage just fine."

Atty smiled.

"You need to give him a break. He really does care for you. He loves you a lot but is concerned. As a father would be. He sees your frustration and wants to help. Sometimes his help, advice may not seem all that perceptive or wise. But if you let it sink in, I think you'd see there is more there than you understand."

"Well, he doesn't bust you the way he does me!"

"Oh, we have our moments. But one thing we both must understand about our father—he is not only very wise, after all he's seen a lot, but he's a pretty gracious, loving, caring, forgiving guy."

"Maybe so. But he just seems to love you more than me sometimes," responded Justus. "I need something from him that he just doesn't seem able to provide."

"Maybe you're asking the wrong questions or making the wrong presentation," said Atty.

Justus, about to respond, cocked his head a bit. His brain - or perhaps it was his heart - seemed to grasp his brother's words. Maybe there *was* something out there for the taking.... if he would just slow down and ask the right question.

*The connection between a father and his son(s) Atticus and Justus is certainly a bit allegorical. There is one wise son who has come to understand how his father truly loves him. Despite having to show discipline at times, his father is quite wise, forgiving and loving. He tries to provide direction, while not failing to point out errors of his sons' ways. Atty gets it. Justus does not. All Justus is focused on is an insatiable drive for success. He thinks he knows what that is. He thinks he knows what will make him happy. But the harder the tries, the more he stumbles to the point of being accusatory to his potential client, brother and even his father. He seems constantly tense (quick handshake instead of a brotherly hug) and agitated (as he enters the coffee shop). Justus is always asking why, why, why. Atty finally turns the tables on him, suggesting that perhaps he is asking the wrong questions. There are definitely times when allowing one's heart to take over a hyper-active brain can bear incredible insight.*

# How a Marriage Should End

**I suspect the title caught your attention. Made you** wonder. "Is there really a 'how to' for ending a marriage?"

Read on. Ending a marriage is not what this is about.

It's actually a story about running. During a time when walls were pressing closer and closer each day during pandemic distancing, many of us pulled out the running shoes and sighed, "At least we can get out and get some exercise."

Some walk. Some run. Some do half-and-half. Having run all my adult life in some fashion, I find those endorphins kind to me even after a couple of miles, sweat pouring down every extremity, my legs aching.

My better half is a runner, too. She's actually more adept than me, having run half marathons in her youth. Single digit body fat. The years have slowed us a bit, but we still enjoy running together.

Well, it's kind of together.

We have a 3.2-mile course we run. We do intervals. Downhill. Uphill. Flats. Run. Walk. Run. Walk. Run. You get the picture. We start out together, but my pace these days is quicker than hers. At the end of the first interval, we face our toughest climb. We slow it down a bit. We talk. And then I'm off again. Run, walk, run until she catches up never having slowed or hastened from her steady pace.

We meet again. And talk some more.

Faster pace from me, steady longer stretches for her. Hills and valleys. Areas where things are flat. As we head back into the neighborhood, she catches me and pulls ahead. I yell encouragement and sometimes tease her. Then I pick up the pace, catch her and we finish together.

And that's the point!

Our running and our marriage are like life. Sometimes the pace is fast. Sometimes it's slow. I charge ahead. She keeps the steady pace. There are hills, valleys, and sometimes long flat stretches. There are times to talk, encourage and tease. There are times to move aggressively forward; times to be a steadying influence. But at the end of the day, we always end at the same point although the effort has been mighty, varied and downright challenging at times.

My wife and I are very different. She thinks with her left brain. I think with my right. I say I'm ready for a run. She says she is, too ...but in 30 minutes. I spend 25 minutes looking at her and wondering. I call something green. She says it's more a blue-gray. I say let's add pepper to a dish, and she says she's already cut them up and put them in. Huh?

I read an article and draw one conclusion. She reads it and draws another. She interprets a scripture verse one way. I see something else. So, we talk about it.

And that's the point!

Despite our differences, we try to find a way to finish together. It's hard, sweaty, grueling work sometimes. But that's how the marriage run should end.

*Marriage is tricky. Thousands of books have been written about it. How to have a successful marriage. How to fix your marriage. How to be more intimate. How to be more understanding. How to take control. Etc. Etc. Etc. It is no doubt the most complex relationship an individual and couple can have. If anyone tells you they've written a book on how easy marriage can be—run! Marriages are not easy. They require a lot of work. The metaphor of running works because it explains that each of the partner's path and run through life is seen differently, approached differently and performed differently. But that's okay. What's vital, however, is that despite the differences, the marriage partners concentrate on coming together at the end of each run, although it is not an easy run sometimes. It requires work and a lot of sweat.*

# An Unexpected Gift

**The week was a long week. Situation after unrelenting** situation. Crises from out of nowhere. Tension. Broken deals. Unsympathetic negotiations. Lethargy. A splitting headache. Sleepless nights.

The walls in my upstairs office crowded me more every day. I needed relief.

Downstairs. Relief was downstairs.

There she was sitting in front of a pair of computers on the make-shift desk of my grandmother's antique secretary. She had been on Zoom calls all morning. There was a problem at her company that needed fixing. She was handling it.

That was her space. Her workspace. I tried not to invade it unannounced. I walked quietly by her to the kitchen.

We'd often laugh as we texted or called each other from a mere 20-plus steps away. Sometimes it was a funny video. Sometimes a text asking when I wanted to run. Another asking what we were having for dinner. Yet another asking what time kickoff was on Saturday and what network was carrying the game.

"I haven't fed the cats, yet," said her text as I entered the kitchen.

I should have known. The furry boys were meowing hangrily. I handled it.

I got another cup of coffee and took one to her. She looked away from the panels, smiled and said thank you. I smiled back. And kept looking at her.

"What?" she asked, as if she had a smudge on her face or a tuft of hair out of place. Although in the era of the home office, none of that really mattered.

But what did matter was that smile in the middle of the day. There have been many of those...accompanied by the long hug in the kitchen for no real reason. The tag team taking out the garbage. Loading and unloading the dishwasher. Searching hopelessly for the TV remote - together. Sharing our social moment of the week by attacking the supermarket in tandem (date night). Fixing dinner together. Deciding on a cab or a pinot. Cramming side-by-side into the tiny laundry room to decide what went into the dryer and what didn't.

And did I mention those long hugs in the kitchen?

There is no question that I knew I loved my wife when I married her. But being able to hang out with her virtually every hour of virtually every day for more than a year has taught me a lot. I don't get tired of her. As a matter of fact, I love being with her more than I ever have. Her smile. Her hugs. Her sometimes weird sense of humor. Her patience with me as she tries to show me the right way to load the dishwasher or sort the laundry.

Sometimes, even when I'm not having a bad day at the office, I simply get up to wander downstairs just to say hi to see how she's doing. Because I've missed her. Crazy, right? I see her more now than I ever have. Yet I miss not being close to her.

But maybe...just maybe...I am closer to her than I've ever been. I am so very thankful for this amazing, unexpected and undeserving gift. The best gifts are like that.

———————✂———————

*I wrote this to coincide with Valentines weekend. I wanted to come up with some way to tell my wife how very much I cared for her, particularly during the craziness and joint solitude of the pandemic. It was an easy write. While we saw a lot of friends, acquaintances, and news stories talking about how frayed relationships were becoming amidst the confinement, our story was nothing like that. We actually grew closer and closer. We laugh that it was probably because we had no choice. But it was genuine. I truly loved having her around constantly. Perhaps it was because for so much of my career and marriage I had traveled. When* you do that, a different mindset takes over. You condition yourself to the gaps that, at times, can create real distance in a marriage. We certainly did not have distance as we worked, ate, slept, cleaned, walked, ran, shopped completely in tandem. And we found that we liked it that way. So, do there need to be gaps in your togetherness as Kahlil Gibran[2] says so well about "On Marriage" in The Prophet? Yes. I think so. But during a wicked time of unpredictability, we clung to each other and began to understand the Oneness of our marriage vows. I believe the scriptures call it "cleave"—to adhere firmly and closely or loyally; unwavering. It's a good thing...as are unexpected and underserving gifts.

# Until Death Do Us Part

**It's 2:30. Middle of the night. Kyle can't sleep. He has not** slept in three days. He's tried. The best he can do are brief cat naps while in his recliner.

He tries to get out of bed. Head to the bathroom. His legs won't cooperate. He grabs the walker nearby. His arms don't have enough strength to lift him from his semi-prone position. He keeps trying. And trying. An hour and a half later, he reaches his destination.

Kyle hasn't always been like this. His voice has softened to where it is sometimes inaudible. His disease has progressed over 18 years. He was not expecting this. But if you asked him, he'd tell you how blessed his life has been.

Wilma is on top of the world. She just got a promotion. She closes her eyes and looks back on her life. Great family. Great schools. Great husband. Great home. And now two wonderful children. She's worked hard for this. She deserves this.

Her husband calls her intense. Everything she does she tackles head-on. Works hard. Plays hard. Devoted to her family. Devoted to her job. "It all kinda works," she claims. High five. Keep the pedal to the floor. Go for it.

One morning, she leaves her house 10 minutes behind schedule. The kids were a bit out of sorts. Required extra time. She's in a hurry. The light turns yellow. She thinks she can make it. She doesn't. The next thing she remembers are sirens.

Luke graduates in a week. Seven long years of college, he laughs, recalling a scene from *Animal House*.[3] But he's made it. A job awaits. The next chapter of his life soon begins. Life in the big city.

Get out the checklist. Find an apartment. Pack. Move. Say good-bye to old friends. Make new friends. Sell the 18-year-old Camry – or perhaps just give it away. It's not worth much. Find new wheels. Impressive ones if possible. The job really is a good one.

He's celebrating his final night in the campus town. He joined friends at a nearby pub. There was a bit of a skirmish. A few of his buds decided to clear out and return to Luke's apartment. The festivities continued. Glasses were raised.

A knock on the door. It was one of them. From the pub. A shot rang out.

Three different people. Different stages of life. Different circumstances. All now fighting for their lives. They never expected this. When does the end come? And why?

Life's guarantee? There really isn't any. Death's guarantee? A reality. But are we ready?

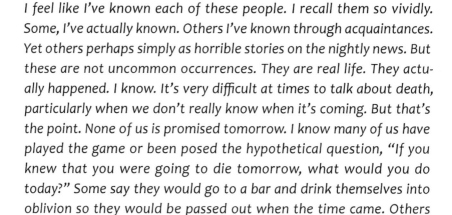

*I feel like I've known each of these people. I recall them so vividly. Some, I've actually known. Others I've known through acquaintances. Yet others perhaps simply as horrible stories on the nightly news. But these are not uncommon occurrences. They are real life. They actually happened. I know. It's very difficult at times to talk about death, particularly when we don't really know when it's coming. But that's the point. None of us is promised tomorrow. I know many of us have played the game or been posed the hypothetical question, "If you knew that you were going to die tomorrow, what would you do today?" Some say they would go to a bar and drink themselves into oblivion so they would be passed out when the time came. Others would throw one last party with friends. Some would go to the most serene place on earth they could get to readily and meditate. Some*

refuse to play. The thought is too daunting for them. Others become incredibly remorseful. Still others speak of sharing their love one last time with those who mean the most to them. The final question posed is worth a serious thought. Seriously.

I had a hard time coming up with a title for some reason. I finally settled on "Until Death Do Us Part," which probably had a lot of readers believing this was going to be about marriage. And metaphorically, maybe it was. A marriage commitment to our heavenly father who can bring us home to join him at any time. If committed. Whether we are ready or not.

While I wanted to present three different people at different stages of their lives facing end-of-the-road circumstances, I wanted their fate to remain the interpretation of the reader. Did they die? Did they survive? If they died, what was their fate? Had they put too much focus on earthly concerns vs. eternal ones? If they lived, how would their life change? Or would it?

With Kyle, he clearly understands that despite his difficult current life, that he has been blessed. Wilma has worked hard and finally achieved seemingly most everything she has wanted and worked for in life. Luke has had less success than Wilma, but he's just starting out and sees nothing but blue sky ahead. Both Wilma and Luke believed they had lots of time left...if they even ever thought of "the end" at all.

How many of us think we have all the time in the world to get things right with God not understanding that the next day is never guaranteed to us. Which begs that final question: Are we ready?

Too often we get caught and seduced by earthly "wins" and believe that winning and success are all that matters... when the real win is understanding that God's grace will provide us eternity with Him if we simply accept, focus and reprioritize.

# The Obit

**I was scanning the obits the other day. I wanted to see** if I was in there...(pause for smile while that sinks in).

Reality is that soon or later, we'll all be "in there."

That doesn't frighten me. I actually look forward to what comes next. Some of you will understand that. Others will not.

Do you ever wonder, though, what will be written about you in those few short paragraphs that attempt to sum up your life? Who will write it? A loved one? The funeral director via his mortuary formula for writing obituaries? How will you be immortalized once and for all? And who will really care what was written a week, a month or a year later?

I came across one the other day that bothered me. It read like a resume. The person wasn't well known but the obit was intent on making the reader feel like that person had contributed greatly to society. It was effusive about all his glowing accomplishments and famous people with whom he had worked.

The gentleman was driven to achieve financial success...achieved tangible results...well-read about businessmen he admired—Sam Walton, Henry Ford, Warren Buffett (all billionaires)... named a company after a similar one founded by Howard Hughes...had ambitious business enterprises...was best remembered for building a massive amusement park (that I never heard of) where he hosted famous country music stars. Unfortunately, the amusement park went under, but he had the business acumen to turn it into an exclusive development to "continue his success."

Don't get me wrong. I find no wrong with earthly success, particularly if we foster the gifts and talents that God gives us. But I was saddened to feel that this man's earthly successes trumped every-thing else.

I don't know how I will be remembered. And I'm not going to write my wish list here. That's for others to decide. But I do hope it will not be for my earthly successes but for those in which I was able to make a difference in people's lives.

Well done, good and faithful servant.

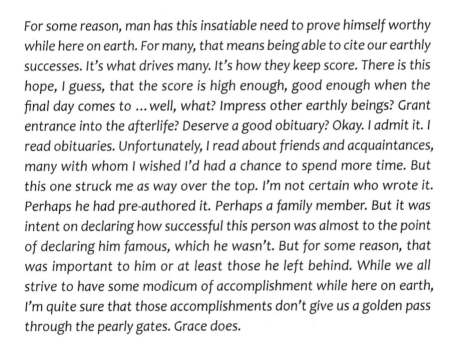

*For some reason, man has this insatiable need to prove himself worthy while here on earth. For many, that means being able to cite our earthly successes. It's what drives many. It's how they keep score. There is this hope, I guess, that the score is high enough, good enough when the final day comes to … well, what? Impress other earthly beings? Grant entrance into the afterlife? Deserve a good obituary? Okay. I admit it. I read obituaries. Unfortunately, I read about friends and acquaintances, many with whom I wished I'd had a chance to spend more time. But this one struck me as way over the top. I'm not certain who wrote it. Perhaps he had pre-authored it. Perhaps a family member. But it was intent on declaring how successful this person was almost to the point of declaring him famous, which he wasn't. But for some reason, that was important to him or at least those he left behind. While we all strive to have some modicum of accomplishment while here on earth, I'm quite sure that those accomplishments don't give us a golden pass through the pearly gates. Grace does.*

# A Tradition Unlike Any Other

**Traditions. There are certain times of year when** traditions begin to kick in. Take Thanksgiving.

I grew up in the country. There were plenty of wide-open spaces. My grandfather's orchard and vegetable farm lay adjacent to our property. Yes, it had pumpkins.

For Thanksgiving, Mom would begin baking early. Apple pies. Pumpkins pies. Perhaps even a cherry pie. And most assuredly a half dozen loaves of homemade bread.

Come Thanksgiving morning, Mom would pick up the pace. She and my sister would be up early while us men folk grabbed our shotguns, camouflage jackets and orange hats. Pheasants and rabbits had no chance against our posse.

By the time we rolled back in mid-day from the frigid fall air, the table was being set, the last pies and dumplings coming out of the oven, and the bird's stuffing beginning to waft through the entire tiny ranch.

As I got older, Thanksgiving Day turned more into Thanksgiving weekend. Visit friends, aunts, uncles, cousins. I came to love the day after Thanksgiving as people shifted into full-blown Christmas mode. A visit to the mall mandatory. Embrace and engulf the chaos. I rarely bought anything. I just wanted to see Christmas begin.

A few years after my daughter was born, the day after Thanksgiving became almost as big as Thanksgiving Day. It was the day we set search for the perfect Christmas tree. We always found it, tied it to the top of the Jeep, and put it up as soon as we brought it into the house.

The lights came first. We laid them out in long lines on the floor, tested to be sure they all worked (they never did), then began wrapping the tree top to bottom. I start on the ladder, handing her the lights as we circled the top of the tree, then finished on the floor, barely reaching each other as the lights came around the tree's fat bottom.

To this day, my daughter is one of the best tree trimmers I know. Perhaps I was a good teacher.

Up until recently, we traveled to my elderly in-laws for Thanksgiving so cousins could do whatever cousins do and family could simply catch up on life. NFL games played quietly in the background. Sadly, that generation is gone, and new traditions are being set.

In 2020, we were not quite sure what to make of Thanksgiving. We hosted. It was a small gathering. Covid tests mandatory to be sure all were safe to enter. Some food was brought, most prepared in the smallish kitchen of our recent downsize.

I ran the city's rescheduled-from-July iconic 10k in the morning. By myself. No jostling between 60,000 of my closest friends along the route. A virtual road race along my personally designed course. Interesting.

We popped open the garage doors, backed the cars out, served the Thanksgiving plates via one server, opened some wine. Then gave thanks in our new open-air venue for a year unlike any other.

A new tradition? Most would probably say, "I hope not." But as we thanked the good Lord for all that he has provided, how he had protected, how he had blessed, we began to realize that 2020 had its strong moments—ones that perhaps we'd taken for granted in the past.

Who knows, in future years we may bring out the masks again as a remembrance for grace among challenges.

*I wrote this a few days before Thanksgiving 2020. While our actual Turkey Day feast didn't exactly match the description, it was close. It was truly a different type of celebration. But celebrate we did. Thankful to be together. Thankful for our health and ability get physical*

*exercise. Thankful for memories and traditions. Thankful for being alive. We often take so much of that for granted during the course of the year, but during the pandemic we learned to take nothing for granted. Many families gathered without members who were there a year earlier. Many families would lose loved ones between this year's celebration and next. Many would become dogmatic as to whether there was need for real concern or not. I continued to see it as part of God's plan to focus on key areas of our lives to which we had not being paying enough attention. If God couldn't get your attention during the pandemic, well, enough said.*

# My Green Truck

**I know. You are probably expecting lyrics for a new** country music song. I may have to actually think about that, but not going there right now.

Life is a teacher. Hmm. Another country song, perhaps.

Each year adds more knowledge and theoretically more wisdom. I sometimes wonder whether more knowledge is good or not. There are some things that I wish I didn't know or see or learn.

As I look back over my youth, I sometimes can't believe I drew some of the conclusions that I did.

Take that green truck. It was a Chevy pickup. When I was learning to drive, it was the teaching vehicle. Three on the tree. I mastered it perfectly and looked forward to graduating to the four-door sedan once I got my license.

Not so fast, my parents said. Until you are 18, you are only allowed to drive the truck.

What?! What about cruising the strip in cool cars? What about taking a carload of buds to the lake (by no means are we going to drink beer)? What about dates?! Ever try making out in the front seat of a truck?

And I guess that was the point. Teenagers think, well, like teenagers.

But as I look back on the wisdom of my parents, I realize that despite all the crazy rules they made—and enforced (my record grounding was two weeks)—they were not only smarter and wiser than me, but they made and enforced those rules because they loved me and wanted to protect me.

Sounds a bit divine, doesn't it?

Life is hard. When we are young, we constantly seem to think, "if I can just get to this stage, this point, this achievement, this age, everything will be better, be okay." But for some reason at each stage, we realize there is still much to learn.

I think that's called growth.

As kids get older, they look at their parents often and think that mom and dad perhaps do have all the answers and have everything figured out. We do a good job of fooling them into thinking that at times.

Every morning when I have my quiet time, I ask for guidance. Because I *don't* have it all figured out. Sure, I believe I'm a bit smarter. I believe I'm a bit wiser. But it's funny how life keeps throwing things at us that we just aren't expecting.

I sure wish I still had that green truck with three on the tree. At least I mastered that.

———————✗———————

*It's interesting what we remember from our childhood. Like that green pickup truck. I'd driven vehicles on the farm—tractors and trucks—since I was 11 or 12. The shifting and the non-power steering didn't bother me. I was "advanced." Or so I thought. I honestly believed that once I got my driver's license that the world would open up to me. Freedom. But Mom and Dad knew a little something about teenage boys and their freedom. Which is why they put clamps on me. Oh sure. I resisted. But those outcomes were never very good and at the end of the day, I always learned something. Mostly that I was wrong, and they were right. And that life would be a lot simpler if I would just listen to them from the start. Ah, the wisdom of parents. The metaphor here is that God and man are like that. He tries to teach. And reach. But often we have preconceived notions of what's best for us. As those notions play out, we realize that He's right and we're wrong. Or at least we should. If not, we stand a really good chance of wrecking that green truck...and our relationship with Him.*

# No One is Tone Deaf...or Please Pass the Salt

**I must admit. Music has never been my strong suit. Oh,** sure. I love to listen. Pandora. iTunes. Apple Music. iHeartRadio. Even sing in the shower. But carry a solid tune? Not so much. I do try to make as joyful a noise as possible.

But singing is not what I'm talking about. I'm talking about *how* we each hear things - from the lips of others.

I contend that no one is tone deaf.

Let's admit it. We all get a little edgy when time is running short or things aren't going well. Deadlines await. Things aren't coming together as they should. Something gets lost that was "just right there." We make a wrong turn. The light turns red a second time before we can get through the intersection - and we were supposed to be there five minutes ago.

Frustration is a part of life. In solitude, any frustrated utterance is merely that. Frustration. No one is really hurt by it except perhaps us as we demonstrate to no one other than ourselves, fortunately, our inability to hold it together.

But what happens when someone else is nearby. Maybe it's simply a stranger. A colleague. A new client. Perhaps it's our kids. Or maybe even someone we care about and love a lot.

Frustration changes our tone of voice. We seldom ever realize it. To hearing ears...it can be painful. Even hurtful. It alters one's opinion of us even if just for an instant. If directed that person's way, he or she may even come back with a cleverly disguised edgy retort of their own...followed by the initiator's not so cleverly disguised next biting round of fodder. . . followed by yet another retort to that retort. Soon the ember is a fire.

It's truly amazing how, "Pass the salt," said in an edgy, snarky way can evolve into, "so you don't like the way I made dinner tonight," to "why can't you ever have dinner ready on time," to "why can't you ever get home on time" to "well, perhaps I won't come home at all."

Okay. That was a pretty fast and irrational progression. (But, hey, this is a thought for everyday living not a short story.) Point is, none of us are immune to having our tone of voice catch someone off-guard. The funny thing is, we hardly ever realize it until the return volley.

In our house, we're trying to get better at that. We attempt to stop the onslaught by having the assaulted one come back as calmly as possible with a smile, perhaps a laugh and a simple utterance of "tone of voice?"

That's the signal that says, "I know you are agitated about something but please don't take it out on me. I love you and want to help if you just give me a chance. But I'm not tone deaf, and that was a bit of a zinger."

"What!?"

Big deep breath.

"So, please pass the salt. Please. Your dinner is amazing."

*The third chapter of James in the New Testament talks about how much irreparable damage can be done by the tongue. Even though it is such a small part of the body, it is as capable as a small spark of setting ablaze great fires. It is described as "restless evil and full of deadly poison." Once those words come out of one's mouth, they cannot be taken back. Sure, apologies and "I'm sorry" may be in order. Some are truly heartfelt. Others merely perfunctory. But even the most heartfelt apologies often are never forgotten if they've cut too deeply into the listener's being and psyche. But the point of this story is that it's not only "what" is said that cuts, it often is "how" one says something that delivers the knockout blow. Snarky. Critical. Cunning. Condescending. Caustic.*

*Cutting. A change of inflection here. An altered pitch there. And before one's brain has caught up with one's mouth, an incredible hurt has been uttered. Some may say, "Oh, don't be such a wimp. Get over it. You're too sensitive. Grow up." Easy admonitions from someone who has likely been hurt by words and who needs and uses such rationale as a defense mechanism for future tongue trashings. I've found those people lash out because they have become used to receiving such admonishment — often from those closest to them. By ones they love. Or wished to. Tone of voice. It can make such a huge difference.*

# The Sunday Drive

**If you are member of the Boomer generation, you** remember Sunday drives. If not, your thoughts might instead go to grabbing that big knocker from your golf bag to launch what is, in your mind, a Tiger Woods-like drive on a Sunday morning.

In the era of quarantines and social distancing the Sunday drive re-emerged. I heard numerous friends —moms and dads at wits end, halfway up the wall —confess to climbing in the car sometimes with their adult kids or rambunctious wee ones on a road to nowhere on a Sunday afternoon.

What are they going to see? Who are they going to visit? Actually, no one. And that's the point. No agenda. Just togetherness. Conversation. Laughter. Games. The alphabet game. "I found an 'X'." And if the tykes are involved, perhaps a bit of hair pulling and good-natured punching.

Sundays were a day of rest when we grew up. Church in the morning. Pot roast and potatoes for lunch. Perhaps an afternoon nap (really!). No work allowed. No mowing the grass much to my delight. But also, no ball games. Bummer. To say my sister and I became a bit restless at times would be an understatement.

Mom and Dad were good at picking up the clues. Dad would back the Chevy out of the garage and give us a choice—wash the car or go for a drive. The car remained dirty.

To say we never really went anywhere would be a serious misnomer because we actually went everywhere and anywhere. A ride through the country, farm after farm along the gently rolling hills. A winding mountain road on the way to our church camp just so we could stick our feet in the pond and hike wooded trails to the top pasture, passing the chapel along the way. A visit on the other side of town to see Grandma or our cousins, so the adults could talk about whatever adults talked about back then while the cousins taught each other things cousins shouldn't be teaching.

At the end of the afternoon, there were two ways home. One was over the mountain where the Christmas Star lit up the sky at Christmas time. The other was through the little town where we went to school. We always rooted for the little town. In that little town was the Swirl, a local soft-serve ice cream parlor. It was a great way to end our Sunday drive.

I'm glad people are rediscovering the Sunday drive. We need to spend more quality time together. There is definite quality in that quality drive.

———————✕———————

*Memories. Fond ones. A time when doing nothing was really everything. A simple ride in the country. With family. With your lover. All alone. For some reason, emotions and senses became heightened as one escaped the drudgeries and demands of the rest of the week. And it really didn't matter where you were going or where you ended up. As a matter of fact, the adventure was really letting it play out. I think we need more moments like that. Fewer plans. More spontaneity. Quality time, indeed.*

# How A Marriage Should End - Part 2

**In my earlier metaphor on marriage, I explained that** when my wife and I run together, we have two different styles and attack the course entirely differently.

In the end, we always make it a point to arrive at the same point at about the same time, albeit one of us a bit more weary or cardio-challenged sometimes.

Part 2. The other day, I decided I was not going to run my pace. I was going to run hers. I was going to stay with her, hang with her the entire way. Change my approach.

What I discovered was a course from a much different perspective. I saw the course the way she saw it, approached hills and valleys and straightaways the way she did, maintained a pace that was, frankly, eye-opening. Easy at times. More difficult than I expected at others.

I came across other runners at different stages of their runs than how and when I normally engaged with them. Some were impediments. Others were near misses as they diverted their course before I could reach them. Yes, there are metaphors here for sure.

My legs and muscles began to hurt in ways they had not hurt or reacted before. I felt the effects for several days after.

But I learned something on that run. I learned the value of staying close to her side. I learned the value of seeing and performing things entirely the way she did—instead of how I did.

Was I a bit grumpy that I was taken out of my comfort zone? Yes. Was I cranky that even several days later, I was still feeling the pain of my altered gait, course and routine? Yes.

But what I learned was invaluable. I learned that while my way of running worked well for me, there were other ways to run the race—ways I had not thought of or paid much attention to. Yes, there was some discomfort involved. But at the end of the run, there we were, recovering together through all the twists and turns, hills and valleys, sprints and stumbles.

I guess that working on relationships sometimes requires changing course, a willingness to see things differently and even withstand some pain at times.

———————✕———————

*The earlier entry concentrated on how one's differences in a marriage or relationship can actually provide it strength. Ying vs. Yang. Strength to complement weakness. Weakness to complement strength. Wisdom to soften foolishness. Foolhardiness to good-heartedly thwart stodginess. But this story addresses the value of trying to see things how our partner sees and approaches things. Often, we are surprised by what we see and learn when we strive to see things through their eyes. We come to understand different perspectives or at least perhaps how to deal with them better. We get closer to understanding how and why our partner operates the way they do. And that's a critical part of a marriage relationship. The effort is not only vital, but it goes a long way to giving us a better understanding of the other...and the capability of loving that person even more once we see what they see.*

# A Knock at the Door

**I sit here in my home office in an affluent American city,** often critical of the way Christianity works—or often doesn't. Meanwhile, news has just broken of a new regime half a world away in a non-Christian country. Many of those not agreeing with the new regime will be captured, tortured, raped and even put to death.

And here I sit.

A friend heads a mission group with many Christian believers in the throes of that government collapse. They do not know what to do. The zealots of the new regime are going door-to-door to identify allies—and those who are not. If you are a follower of Christ, you are not. You are dead.

And here I sit.

It's almost time for lunch. Perhaps I'll go downstairs and make a sandwich. Flip on the TV. See the latest on the collapse.

Some of the images are disturbing. Some make me feel a bit uncomfortable. I turn to ESPN. There. That's better.

I begin to beat myself up a little for not continuing to follow the chaos. But hey, what can I do? I don't understand international policy. I don't understand the lifestyle over there. And I surely don't understand their religion—or lack of one.

So here I sit.

I say to myself, "Well, you can always pray." So, I do. But that only helps me feel less guilty.

I begin to wonder what it would feel like. What would it be like to have someone knock on my door and ask me what I believed? My wife and kids secure in another part of my house, or so I think, I utter some nebulous double-speak answer.

A gun is put to my head. Four men rush into my home. They find my wife. They find my son. They find my daughter. They are brought to me. Still standing at the front door. With a gun to my head. Every one of my family has a long knife at their throats.

I am told to bow to a foreign god and swear allegiance to him or I will watch my family die.

"Are you a Christian?" one of the men shouts.

I pause. I look at my wife. My son. My daughter.

A knife makes the first cut.

I fall to my knees.

"God forgive me."

I come out of my stupor. I go back to my office upstairs. I pray. So hard that tears begin to fall. Is that enough? Is that all I can do?

I don't know. And that's what makes this so hard. A bit too critical? Perhaps. But deservedly so. In that country halfway around the world, there are 20,000 Christians prepared to die. They will not deny their faith.

What would *I* do?

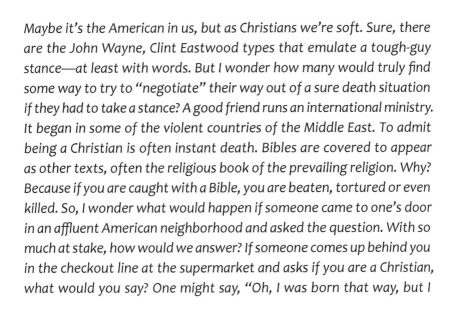

*Maybe it's the American in us, but as Christians we're soft. Sure, there are the John Wayne, Clint Eastwood types that emulate a tough-guy stance—at least with words. But I wonder how many would truly find some way to try to "negotiate" their way out of a sure death situation if they had to take a stance? A good friend runs an international ministry. It began in some of the violent countries of the Middle East. To admit being a Christian is often instant death. Bibles are covered to appear as other texts, often the religious book of the prevailing religion. Why? Because if you are caught with a Bible, you are beaten, tortured or even killed. So, I wonder what would happen if someone came to one's door in an affluent American neighborhood and asked the question. With so much at stake, how would we answer? If someone comes up behind you in the checkout line at the supermarket and asks if you are a Christian, what would you say? One might say, "Oh, I was born that way, but I*

*really don't go to church anymore." Or, "That's an interesting question. Why do you want to know?" Or, "Yes, I am. How did you know?" We're getting closer. In many areas of the world, the wrong answer makes for a short life. In America, we often figure a way to dance around the question not realizing our feeble but more comfortable answer still costs us our life—eventually.*

# My Brother

**A war in a distant land raged. Many protested. And** showed their own rage against that napalm-infused country half a globe away. Others protested against the protesters. God and country were alive and should be honored and exulted. We can never give up the ship and let our principles and government be tarnished was their mantra.

For every song against the war like "For What It's Worth" written by Steven Stills and recorded by Buffalo Springfield, there was a song supporting our warriors like "Ballad of the Green Berets" written and performed by Staff Sergeant Barry Sadler.[4] There didn't seem to be a middle ground.

And then along came "He Ain't Heavy, He's My Brother." Written by Bob Russell and Bobby Scott, it seemed to speak to both extremes. The protesters claimed everyone, every race, was our brother and we had to do what we could to help that person. His problems and differences weren't too heavy for us. His issues were something we needed to embrace and help him through.

The loyalists, either actually or viscerally, saw and tasted the blood that was shed in battle. It was a brutal war. Nearly 60,000 died. Horribly at times. What is not horrible about a life taken far too young? And for what? But when you are in a foxhole and your mate, who has gone through training with you, waded through rice paddies with you and dodged bullets with you, goes down...you pick him up. Your only thought is that "I must save his life." He is not too heavy to carry out. He is my brother.

I love this song. It speaks to me. It did back then. It still does today. Perhaps even more so because much of the strife and extremes of that era are still with us.

The road is indeed long with many winding turns to which we know not where it will end. But it will end. Yet, somewhere along the way, we are guaranteed tough times. Who is going to be there to help us through those tough times?

As we look across the room, into the eyes of another, what do we see? What trouble lies behind those eyes. What is the struggle within? What burden does he have that I can share with him? And be glad to do it. Because I love my brother.

A lawyer once asked Jesus to explain who exactly *was* his neighbor when told to love his neighbor as himself. The great teacher told the story of the Good Samaritan, a man of another race, religion and culture that saved and cared for a Jewish man who had been beaten and bloodied, left for dead.

Brotherhood knows no boundaries. His burden is not too heavy to share. To carry. His well-being is my concern. I am glad to share his burden and grateful he will help me bear mine.

# He's not heavy. He's my brother.

*The road is long*
*With many a winding turn*
*That leads us to who knows where*
***Who knows where***
*But I'm strong*
*Strong enough to carry him*
*He ain't heavy, he's my brother*

*... So on we go*
*His welfare is of my concern*
*No burden is he to bear*
***We'll get there***

*... For I know*
*He would not encumber me*
*He ain't heavy, he's my brother*
*... If I'm laden at all*
*I'm laden with sadness*
*That everyone's heart*
**Isn't filled with the gladness**

*Of love for one another*
*... It's a long, long road*
*From which there is no return*
*While we're on the way to there*
**Why not share**

*... And the load*
*Doesn't weigh me down at all*
*He ain't heavy he's my brother*
*... He's my brother*[5]

– The Hollies
(Bob Russell, Bobby Scott)

———————◇———————

Brotherhood. It's a word, a concept, that is thrown around a lot these days. Sports teams, fraternities, even corporations that profess a social consciousness embrace the term. I question its authenticity. And there is nothing wrong with such a query. Until one understands the true and complete sacrifice one has to make to truly put someone else's situation—someone else's being, someone else's life—before theirs, they aren't getting it. The gospel of John says that there is no greater love than to lay down one's life for his brother. His friends. Wow. That's a lot to ask, you may say. But to understand the true meaning of brotherhood: caring for a person's well-being over yours, grieving with him, celebrating with her - that concept not only has to be understood, but taken to heart. Because it is changes of the heart that result in changes in character. Not the head.

# Family Man

**He was a business owner. A family man. A Little League** coach. A scout master. A deacon at his church. A leader of a discipleship group. A master barbecue chef to his neighborhood group.

I tried to be impressed as he rattled them all off.

"What about you?" he asked in such a way that I could tell he was relishing a comparison.

"I just try to be a humble servant and let the good Man open doors," I answered. I didn't feel like being baited.

"Well, that sounds rather nebulous," he replied. "So where are you taking me for lunch."

"Oh, I've got this place over in Shantytown that has super soul food. You'll love it."

"Whoa. Shantytown? I really don't hang there much. Not very safe if you know what I mean."

"It's fine. I go there often when I'm near that area of town. The people are great and the food amazing. Get to start good conversations sometimes, too."

We walked in. I could tell he was more than nervous when he pushed down the lock button on his passenger door as we entered the neighborhood.

"Dude," he protested. "We're the only white people in here."

"Really? Imagine that."

Clarence the restaurant owner came over and gave me a big hug.

"How ya' doing, brother?" he asked.

"Better once I get some collards and cornbread in front of me."

We both laughed. I introduced him to my friend. Clarence chided him for hanging out with me, but said he was holding my usual booth for me.

"Right next to my cousin, Jerome. He just got in last night from the Delta."

I asked Jerome if he wanted to join us. He graciously accepted and slid into the booth right next to my friend. Jerome was wired. He liked to talk almost as much as Clarence.

"So, I know about this guy from Clarence, but what about you?" he asked my friend. "Tell me about you. What do you do?"

My friends eyes were casing the place. Small beads of sweat began to appear on his brow.

"Excuse me. Can you say that again?"

"Whatsamatter?" Jerome laughed. "Don't hang out in these parts much?"

"Not really," was the understated reply. "I live a good ways from here."

"Ok, let's start there. Where do you live?"

My friend named the suburb.

"Whoa. Nice. Great digs from what I've seen driving through there," effused Jerome. "Do you play golf? Are you a member of the club there?"

My friend was surprised Jerome knew so much about his home turf.

"Well, yes. But that's not all I do."

"So, back to the original question. What do you do?"

My friend rattled off the litany. Business owner. Little League coach. Scout master. Deacon. Discipleship leader. Barbecue chef extraordinaire.

"Wow. A real family man," proclaimed Jerome. "How big is your company?"

"We're small firm. About a hundred people. But we do nearly 50 million in revs."

"That's great—a real opportunity to give back to the Lord and the community. What type of things do you like to give to?"

My friend was becoming a tad uneasy.

"It depends. Varies from year-to-year," was his response.

"So, tell me—how many Black people do you have at your company?"

My friend did not see that one coming.

"I think maybe four or five. We'd like to have more. Just can't find the skill set."

"Really? Interesting. So how many Black kids do you have in your Little League and in scout troop?"

"Uh, we have one Hispanic on the Little League team," replied my friend. The sweat on his brow was becoming more profuse.

"Okay. Well, that's a start. But you do realize that a Hispanic is Brown, not Black. But it's a start."

He paused. "Tell me about your last neighborhood cookout. I love cookouts."

Now my friend was getting more back in his wheelhouse.

"Man, we had nearly 40 people from the neighborhood. It was great. Great music. Games. The kids playing frisbee, soccer, pitch-and-putt. And my ribs and 'cue were out of this world. I have a special sauce I make myself."

"Sounds terrific. I'd like to come next time I'm in town. How many people like me?"

"From the Delta?" my friend asked in complete naivety.

"No, Black folk. How many black folk come to your cookouts?"

"Well, we really don't have any. They just don't live in our neighborhood. It's mostly church members. Some really fine folk."

"I see. I'm beginning to get a better picture. Thanks for sharing."

The collards, cornbread and barbecue arrived.

"So how would you compare this 'cue to yours," I asked my friend.

"Different," was the reply.

Yes. Different indeed.

---------------⋈---------------

*Too many of us live in our own unconscious worlds with our own unconscious biases. That for which we strive the most is comfort. It's not wealth. Or security. Or a beautiful, handsome spouse. Or a well-decorated house. Or respectful kids. Or even accolades. Because all those things give us comfort. With that comfort, we convince ourselves everything is all right and just as God wants it to be. So, we either will* not or choose not to see things around us that are obvious to others, most often those whose circumstances and experiences have been anything but comfortable. Jesus dragged his disciples into some very uncomfortable places. Those with diseases. Prostitutes. The poor. The extravagantly wealthy. The antagonistic. Those who didn't look like him. Because that's where he was most comfortable. You say, "Sure, but that was his job." But to whom did he leave that job? One learns very little about life if constantly surrounded by comfort.

GIVING

# Where There's a Will

*I have a new friend. I'll call him Will. I'd like him to tell* you his story.

I grew up in rural Alabama. There was Mom, Dad, my sisters Lisa and Lakisha, and me. Plus, our dog, Malvern. I'm not sure why we named him Malvern. Someone said that was the name of our mailman, and he always chased the postal truck. So, I guess he got named after our mail carrier. For a long time when I was younger, I thought his name was Malvern No. But then I caught on.

I caught on to a lot of things at an early age. My mom was a teacher's assistant. She only had an associate's degree, so the school district would only allow her to "assist" in the classroom. She was sharp as a whip though. It wasn't her fault that her parents could not afford full-blown college.

My dad worked at the local textile mill. He started sweeping floors at age fourteen and worked his way up to the dye bleaching machines before they moved him to shipping. He bragged that he was the best dye bleacher on the floor, but they told him that dye bleaching was better suited for the women folk, and his brawn was needed in shipping.

One day, a few of the drivers didn't show up. They asked Dad to make a run to Birmingham. He never made it back. An 18-wheeler hit him head-on.

That was rough, but Mom, Lisa, Lakisha, and me pieced things together the best we could. We all got part-time jobs to help pay the bills. We tried best we could to put some money away for college. Mom was determined for us to go even though she knew we would probably have to rely on loans, financial aid, and such.

I was the youngest, so Lisa and Lakisha got first crack. They made the most of it, but money ran out for both somewhere around the second and third year. They picked up a retail job or two in Birmingham and eventually moved into a one-bedroom apartment together, pinching pennies, dimes, and quarters.

I wanted to stay near home to help Mom. I told her that I thought the local community college would work out great. I could get a two-year degree and still be around enough to help her.

She wouldn't hear of it.

"Will," she said to me, "you are the best student of my beloved three, and I don't want to see you get stuck like I have with just a two-year degree. We'll find a way to get you through."

She was right. I did have very good grades. I applied to several state schools but my guidance counselor thought I should aim big—Georgia Tech.

Ex-pen-sive! Whew.

But he told my mom and me that there would be quite a bit of financial aid. And there was. But not quite enough.

At home, jobs were drying up which meant fewer families in the county. That meant fewer students. That meant less need for teachers and teacher's assistants. My mom lost her job. Then our house burned, and we had to move in with my cousin's step-sister. We didn't know her and her boyfriend very well. But they were nice to take us in.

I told mom I wasn't going to leave her, but when the acceptance letter came from Georgia Tech, she told me I could under no circumstances not go. She called it God's will and that I couldn't go against God's will. How was I to argue with that?

Money was still tight, but I figured I could make it work if I took just enough hours to maintain my financial aid package, found cheaper housing, and worked a few odd jobs.

It seemed like a good plan at first, but I was having a hard time making enough money for the rent split with the five other guys in the rented house. I found a very small studio in a not-so-great part of town, but I couldn't afford all the utility and internet hookups.

So, I decided to live out of my car for a while. It's been six months now. Mom doesn't know I'm living in my car and few of my classmates or teachers have figured it out either. But I can't keep going on like this. I need to find a place that's safe and secure. The stress is taking its toll on my grades. And I have to find a way to help mom.

Yeah, I know it's hard to believe that a college kid could actually be homeless. But I am. It sucks.

Homelessness tugs at my heart more than about anything. It just isn't fair. We live in one of the most advanced and affluent societies in the entire world, yet millions live in poverty. Many homeless.

My daughter spent a Thanksgiving with me one year not so long ago. We had a great Italiano celebration at one of the city's well-noted Italian restaurants. The helpings were gargantuan. About halfway through the meal, we looked at each other, realizing we could never finish. We asked for doggie boxes. Then headed downtown to the inner city in search of those not able to be all that thankful that day.

Living in a metropolitan area, one is periodically approached by someone on the street in need of money. Many are homeless. Friends tell me, "Don't fall for it. They're just looking for drug or alcohol money." That may be the case. But maybe it's not. Maybe they are truly in need. I often try to engage them in a conversation. "What's going on? What's your story? Where do you go for help? Where do you sleep at night?" I ask them if they know why I'm helping them. Most just look at me. I tell them it's because God wants me to help and, that God loves them. Get close to Him if they can. The conversation never really gets beyond that, but I'd like to think that somewhere over the last many years that the message sunk in with at least one. And his life got better. If the message goes in one ear, out the other, and they walk to the nearest liquor store, well, shame on them. I've at least planted a seed.

In Matthew, Jesus says that if you ignore those in need, you've ignored him as well. "Whatever you did not do for one of the least of these, you did not do for me."[6]

The genesis on this story was a phone call from friend and colleague Bob Hope, former public relations guru and board member of the Atlanta Braves. Bob's heart for the homeless beats much like mine. One day he called and asked if I would be interested in being on call with The Covenant House. The Methodist-associated ministry operates a homeless center for young people. It runs an annual fund-raiser in which it attempts to raise $1 million for homeless youth, culminating with a Sleep Out in the inner city with some of the home's residents. I was all-in. There were so many touching stories. I asked to speak to one of the young people so I could share his or her story, but the Covenant House wanted to maintain privacy for the young people. I understood. But by that time, I had heard enough of them share their stories that I felt I could assemble many of their circumstances into one story. So that's what I did.

# Everyone Loves Money

**Money. Everyone loves money. And although our pastors** tell us that the love of money is the root of all evil, we smile. And rationalize.

I mean, how bad can money be? We need it to put food on the table, gas in the car, clothe ourselves, pay the mortgage, make the car payment, go out to eat, take a vacation, pay the utility/cable/cell phone bills, furnish the house, landscape the yard, pay college tuition, buy pet food, pay the doctor and the vet, and oh yeah—make contributions to charities or our church if there's enough left over.

We may have that backward.

Perhaps we should think about making that contribution first and then see what's left for the remaining accoutrements. I call them "accoutrements" because much of that above list is not really necessary—at least to the degree that many believe.

We are a nation oft called the greatest nation on earth, yet we struggle greatly with poverty, hunger, inequality and pervasive indifference.

Since the 1970s, the income gap in America has grown dramatically. In the last fifty years, the average income of the low and middle class has risen 12 percent, while the average income for the wealthy, or what I call the "C-suiters," has risen 940 percent.[7] Great for the C-Suiters. Not so much for the rest of the populace.

But we all like money, right? So, what do we do to fix this dilemma? Do we simply throw all the money into a pile in the middle and tell everyone to "have at it?" Or do "haves" figure out a way to reach out and help the "have nots?"

Charitable and faith-based giving is a great way to do that. Unfortunately, in what is called perhaps the greatest economy on earth (debatable, I know), Corporate America gives only 0.8 percent of its earnings to charity, while individuals only 2.1 percent.[8] So much for the concept of tithe (10 percent).

Okay. We can do better. But what do we have to do; what do we have to ask ourselves in order to actually...do better?

Well, let's look at that list of "accoutrements."

Food on the table? Pretty much a necessity, but how many of us over-buy or put items in the cart that may comfort and please us, but really aren't necessary or even that healthy.

Gas in the car? Do we really need that gas-guzzling eight-cylinder SUV or could an EV get us to work, the store, church and back just as well?

Clothes? How full are your closets? And how many brand labels are there? What if instead of spending $5,000 a year on clothes, you only spent half that and gave the other half to a local shelter?

The Mortgage? How many of those living in $1 million-plus homes could actually live comfortably in a still very nice $500,000 home? That would allow you to give a half million away or at least the difference of your monthly mortgage payment to charity. I know. Some people like to brag about the size of their mortgage payment. Get over it!

The car payment? This one befuddles me. For the life of me, I can't understand why someone would pay $60,000, $80,000, even $100,000 for a vehicle to get them from Point A to Point B when one costing half or a quarter of that would accomplish the same thing. Next time you're tempted to buy the $80,000 foreign model, trying giving $40,000 away and buy the more-than-adequate $40,000 American model. Some of them are pretty nice, and it pays to buy American. Plus, you will probably save a lot on insurance and maintenance as well. Even more money to put in that charity till.

Go out to eat? The expense *really* adds up unless you are hitting MICKEY D'S™ or my favorite, CFA®. A decent meal at a sit-down restaurant with adult beverages, tax and gratuity can easily reach $150 per couple. If you do that once a week (and some do even more), try cutting back to twice a month and give the other half of those funds to the homeless shelter.

Vacation? During a time when more socializing was the norm, I would show up at a party and, invariably, everyone wanted to talk about where they were going on vacation or where they had been. Europe. Bahamas. Skiing in the Rockies. California wine country. Coastal resort. Thailand. Or perhaps just Myrtle Beach. Some were easily dropping $10,000 every time they did a getaway junket "just to get away from all the stress."

Utility, cable, cell phone? There are all sorts of ways to cut these costs, but for some it's hard not to have the latest and greatest gadget or technology. Bragging rights to some. Bragging rights come at a cost. Some of those could go to the giving account.

Furnished, professionally decorated house or landscaped yard? We all should take pride in keeping our residence "kept," a.k.a. clean and tidy. But I never understood why someone buys the $1,500 lawn mower when the $350 lawnmower cuts the grass just as well (ok, perhaps it takes longer). Or the $2,000 grill over the $299 model. Or the $25,000 dining room suite over the $4,500 one. Some argue that the more one pays, the better quality one gets. Really? I'm not sure Consumer Reports agrees. For some, I suspect it's appearances and more bragging rights.

Pet food/vet? We all love our pets. But my wife queries me whenever we go out of town about paying a pet sitter or housing at the kennel. Those couple of hundred dollars add up. And man, Fluffy and Brutus' doctor bills are sometimes higher than ours. But yes, they are like family. So, you do it. Even if you have to cut into your church tithe that month. Hmmm.

College tuition? There is a wide spectrum here and thankfully, many different ways to cover college costs from scholarships to grants to work study programs. I do remain amused, however, at parents who willingly brag about how much it's costing them to send their child to one of the elite colleges. Dollar for dollar, I'm pretty convinced those elites are not worth it.

That pretty much falls into the same category as private K-12 school. Talk about developing a child with a sense of entitlement. Whoa. A waste! I know. I sent mine. Thirteen years at about a quarter-million dollars. She never made it past a year and a half in college. Her real education came via the School of Hard Knocks. There will be plenty of those. She's doing quite well. Meanwhile, what I missed was the chance to give a quarter-million dollars to an organization that could have really used it or even saved a little for a rainy day.

Some of you may think I'm being overly critical. But trust me, I've lived that life. And come to understand that things, appearances, and bragging rights don't make one happy. I'm a lot happier trying to find ways to help those less fortunate and don't mind cutting a few financial corners to do that.

Okay. Every once in a while, I'll pay full price for a tub of Ben & Jerry's.

————✗————

*This is one of the longest entries. I am struck by how much excess there is—particularly among the affluent. And as the pandemic took its toll on more and more lives and livelihoods, I kept feeling like the "haves" really needed to step up and help those in need. Yet, I was seeing and reading about the rich getting richer and how their affluence was allowing them to keep their distance from the virus simply by buying their way away from it—trips to secluded resorts, fancy motorhomes, special cleaning services, private deliveries, private parties.*

*Over the last several years, I've learned how to live on a lot less. I've had to. And ya' know, I've come to realize that a lot which I thought I needed, I simply wanted. I didn't really need as much as I thought I did. Meanwhile, people were going hungry, losing jobs and businesses, being evicted, needing clothing, and a host of other things about which the affluent had no inkling.*

*As I looked at all the things I have personally spent money on, I was ashamed. I wanted readers to know that THIS WAS NOT NECESSARY. Reading between the lines, I was hoping readers would say, "Ok, I can't* go to restaurants like I used to because of the pandemic, so how can I spend that extra 'white table cloth' money?" Give. It. Away.

Years ago, the letters "WWJD" were all the rage in the Christian community. What Would Jesus Do? Well, I think Luke 12:48, tells us exactly what He would do.

*To whom much is given, much will be required.*

# Mustang and Sally

**Summertime and the livin' wasn't easy. I was between** my sophomore and junior year in college and running the family business. A farm. The summer was hot. Early mornings. Long days. I longed for just a simple respite.

After dinner one evening, I pulled an escape. I hopped in the family pickup and ended up gazing at her. There she stood. In the middle of an array of other outstanding species. She was golden brown. And she was beautiful. The most beautiful Mustang I'd ever seen.

Sleek. Stylish. Fast.

Three-speed on the floor. V8 engine. Bucket seats. If I couldn't impress with her, I was not breathing.

It's funny about boys and their toys. There seems to be a psyche and testosterone boost that comes with anything that makes them feel important. Successful. Gladiator-like. My Mustang, my first ever set of wheels came with all that.

As I wheeled my way onto campus that fall, I could see eyes turn as I rounded the corner to the student center. And there was Sally. We had met the prior spring. Dated. Kinda liked each other. Wrote to each other daily throughout the summer.

Yes. She was impressed.

We rolled the windows down so our hair could blow as we waved to our admiring onlookers. I was on top of the world. Amazing what a hot set of wheels and a beautiful 20-year-old can do for one's ego.

As I got older and the career roared into full bloom, that calling to great cars continued. Afterall, they evoked status. If your career was on the rise, you had a certain image to project and protect. Image was important. Perception was if you dressed great and drove a cool car, you must have something going for you. An impressive logo on your business card helped too.

Sally and I married. Hit a wall. Career crashed.

As my life reconstructed, I somehow found myself around cars again. Fast cars. Cars that raced and made the nightly news. Expensive cars.

Expensive cars bring clients with expensive tastes and all too often unrealistic and tragic views about life. I came not to enjoy those cars so much anymore.

I was often asked by my well-coiffed clients, what type of car I drove. I'd tell them a rental car. I traveled non-stop and had no need for a car. They found that amusing but entirely incomprehensible. When goaded as to how often I rented a Corvette or Porsche, I rolled my eyes, said "never," and changed the topic—often leading to conversations about their wine cellar or their next trip to the Islands, Europe or wherever.

Now, don't get me wrong. I certainly appreciate the styling, design and technical innovation that goes into an automobile. I learned a lot about that. I had to. But to me, a car now is nothing more than transportation to get from Point A to Point B—transportation for which one must pay insurance, maintenance, repairs and gas. A depreciating asset. No need to spend the equivalent of a small mortgage on a depreciating asset. Seems rather wasteful and silly quite frankly.

Oh, by the way. That sleek college-bound Mustang. It took forever to sell once it got some age and miles on her. Came with no air conditioning. Seduced by the outside without understanding the inside, including no comprehension about Southern temperatures and humidity.

Wouldn't it be great if we spent our time and money on what is really necessary rather than what we believe we need for people to form certain opinions of us? There are a lot of things that fall into that category, I guess.

———————⋈———————

It's interesting to look back on one's youth and see how impressionable one was. Being liked. Making a good impression. Having fun. All are paramount. I'd like to say that we all eventually outgrow that insatiable desire, but I'm afraid many don't. The need to impress drives many throughout their lifetimes. It's how they strive to get jobs. Girlfriends. Boyfriends. Wives. Husbands. Promotions. Attention. Accolades. While none of those are necessarily evil aspirations, the key question becomes motivation. Are you doing it for yourself? To pump yourself up? To give yourself confidence? Self-esteem? Showmanship? Or is your motivation realizing that God has given you incredible gifts and talents and by not using them for how and what He wants you to use them is cheating Him and you. If it's the latter, God bless. If making an impression is driving you...good luck. At the end of the day, you will have a lot of questions to answer.

# Puppy Love

**No. Not what you think.**

This is about business. All about business. And business is all about making money. Right?

Economist Milton Friedman strongly suggested that a corporation's role was to put the shareholder first. That meant maximizing returns and making money. He left no room for corporate social responsibility. As a matter of fact, he deemed it detrimental to corporate growth.

As most of us sat home behind PC and Zoom screens during the pandemic, we came to understand there were ways to do business that we never before could have imagined. The last decade or so has thrown us a great recession, a pandemic, another recession, isolation and a lot of queries about how business works.

Businesses have been lost. Jobs have disappeared. Savings and 401k's ravished. Our health has been put in jeopardy by more than a virus. We look for mental, emotional, spiritual relief. We are exhausted. There had to be help on the way... or else.

But an odd thing happened on the way to the funny farm. We began to see some good. We saw neighbors helping neighbors. Learning about them. Learning, perhaps who our neighbor actually was. And he/she didn't have to look like us, think like us, be like us or even want like us. We just knew that there were people out there who were having a hard time getting through life, whether that was corporate life or personal life.

So, we began to think less about our own plight and more about the needs of our brothers and sisters, mothers and fathers, sons and daughters, next-door neighbors, and even that person on the TV screen to whom we knew we had to find a way to reach...somehow. Because we wanted to help.

I think God programs most of us that way. The choices we make, however, are up to us. Too often, it takes catastrophe and tragedy to wake us up. Sadly, we need that sometimes.

I once worked for an entrepreneur who was maniacal about the bottom line. He struggled to balance it. Keep it in the black. He tried all sorts of schemes. And many were just that. Schemes. Falsely hidden with hope and superlatives when they were anything but. The whole focus was blackening that bottom line no matter what.

I once suggested that aligning with a key charity or two might be a good way to make the business look more human. Look like we actually cared about something humane in addition to maximizing returns and making money. My argument was that in an era of corporate responsibility, many corporate partnerships can be forged with companies who are like-minded, cause driven.

The rather heated reply was, "If we start aligning with charities and non-profits, we will become one ourselves. And you like to be paid, don't you?"

"You know the problem with you," he continued. "You have this penchant for picking up every stray dog or puppy who needs help. I don't need any dogs or puppies. I need a goose that will lay the golden egg. Now, go find one of those for me."

Basically...toe the line or look elsewhere.

The decision was easy. I love puppies. I chose the puppy.

I think that puppy came back to bite him.

*Yes, I take an early swipe at monetarism. Ronald Reagan was a huge fan of Friedman's and the trickle- down economy. Forty years later, as the wage, wealth and home ownership gap widened, it was easy to see that wealth was not trickling down. The rich were getting richer. To take some of the heat off, corporations devised corporate social responsibility programs and departments. Many made impactful contributions*

to charitable causes and marginalized peoples. But at the end of the day, corporate giving averaged a mere single percentage point of its overall spend, while corporate executives became millionaires via generous stock and option plans—whether the company was exceeding expectations or not. Charitable giving certainly makes Corporate America seem more human. Far too many, however, hold their noses realizing it's good PR but inwardly feel, like Friedman, that it is not good business. And some, like my one-time boss, had no interest in giving back. At least he didn't play the game and pretend to be a good guy.

# Checklist

**How many of you are checklist people?**

Guilty! I start the day with a checklist. I end the day with a checklist. I modify that list all day long. I convince myself that it keeps me organized and sane.

After I make the list, I read through it and begin to prioritize things. At the beginning of the day, I number them in the order I wish to attack the tasks at hand. But I've noticed something recently. The low numbers, which are where I begin, are often the tasks that I can knock out the quickest. I rationalize that I'm making progress if I get a whole bunch of items off that list early.

That keeps me happy, in a good mood.

If I can accumulate a certain number of check marks by a certain time mid-morning, I convince myself that my day is off to a good start. And woe to any unexpected caller who dares disturb my rhythm and roll.

As I take my first break, I look at what remains and tell myself I really need another cup of coffee before I begin yet another assault on the list. Caffeine kicks in. I'm off and running. A pair of Zoom calls, a battering of emails needing a response, even more to glance at and delete. Some to save for later. Just don't have time. Maybe end of day. Maybe quickly print an article to read later so I don't accidently delete it.

Oh my gosh. It's lunch time. Make it fast. I had to add quite a few things to my list over the last couple of hours and now—oh, no!—I could be running behind the rest of the day.

What's more important? Those things I added? A pair of proposals facing deadline? That missed call for which I've been waiting two weeks? What about that SOS from my friend whose voice seemed to crack with need?

Uh oh. The day is starting to spin out of control. Big breath. Say a prayer. There, that's better.

Drat, just missed another important call. And when did these three texts come in? Where's my list?!

Sounds a bit frantic, doesn't it? It can be. Particularly if we choose to live and die by how many items we can check off our list rather than understand what true progress may entail.

At the end of the day, especially a particularly crazy one, I often look at that list and try to tell myself that I've had a good day or a bad day simply by looking at the amount of check marks.

But have I?

What really matters —did I make a difference in anyone's life today? Did I call back that friend whose voice cracked with need? Too often I don't like that answer.

Maybe my first entry on that checklist every day should be just that: **Make a Difference Today.**

———————✕———————

*If ever I was pointing a finger at myself, this was it. For way too long, that was how I operated every day. I set out with that to-do checklist and marched as methodically through it as I could. When things began to get out of kilter, there went my day. Bad day. Mr. Grumpy Pants. But I'm gradually pulling away from that. It has taken time. One doesn't turn the corner immediately. But I'm learning that if I get to the end of the day or even allow it to spill over into the early morning hours of my quiet time, I at least begin to ask the right questions. What happened today? Why didn't things go the way I planned? And more importantly, what did I learn today? The answers don't come quickly. They can't. If they are that easy to answer, I could fix everything on a moment's notice. But I can't. I need to be still. I need to listen. I learn that many of the things I believe to be important are not all that important to God. And even if they are, His timing may not coincide with my timing. I know* who wins out there. So, I question. I listen. And the answer comes back the same—*Make a Difference for Me Today.* I just need to learn how to interpret that and how to implement it. For that I need grace, wisdom and understanding. And I can't manufacture that myself.

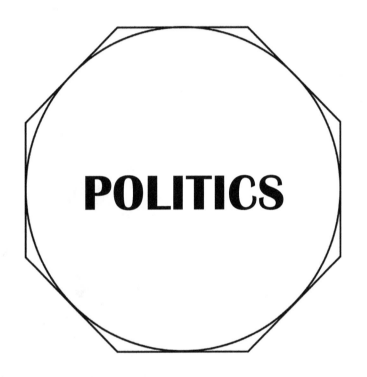

# POLITICS

# Bridge Builder

**With a degree in the humanities, I never really considered** a career in architecture. My brain just isn't wired that way.

Ya' know, it's funny though. Sometimes the humanness of the humanities syncs with building.

I'm talking about building bridges. Oh, not the Golden Gate or Brooklyn or London kind. Human bridges.

I had a conversation with someone the other day. The person was a bit irritated with the state of recent elections. I patiently listened.

I then tried to explain how so very important it is to build bridges not walls...even between people who might not always see eye-to-eye.

He was having none of it.

He asked when any of "my people" were known to have built bridges.

"My people?" I'm wasn't quite sure where he was coming from, or even going for that matter. So, I asked. And then provided a bit of emphasis.

"By 'my people' do you mean whites, Christians, or my family's immigrant history from Europe? Not quite sure in what context to put your question, but here's my take. . .

"Building bridges is essential to create unification in this country.

"When we can create an economy that works for all people not just an elite few, we begin to build bridges.

"When we create an education system that gives the impoverished and minorities a real chance to make their lives better, we build bridges.

"When we have a healthcare system that works for the entire population no matter what age, color or societal class, we build bridges.

"When we begin to clean up a dirty environment that has the potential to wreak havoc across all sectors, we build bridges.

"When we recognize systemic racism and say I'm going to teach my kids a different way, a way to reach out, lift up, love and treat all people the same, we build bridges.

"When we teach that homophobia is *not* okay and that God loves all people, we build bridges.

"When we see immigrants of all nationalities coming to America because they still believe it is the land of opportunity, and we go out of our way to prove to them that it actually is, we build bridges.

"I haven't seen much of that in the last few years. We need to get back there."

He thought for a while.

"Yeah, well good luck with that. All sounds great, but not very realistic."

I suspect that he would not have been a very good architect.

No question that the 2020 presidential election was contentious—the most contentious of any since I became of voting age. Innovation in the form of social media contributed to much of that. Okay. I'll go a step further—most of that—as people expressed wild opinion after unfettered opinion behind the cloak of secret handles, accounts and organizations to express unsubstantiated viewpoints. I refuse to call them reason.

It seemed as if the country was coming apart at the seams at times. The extremes on many positions were mind-boggling. How did we get here? Could we not somehow agree on the easy-to-identify problems and find ways to try to fix them together?

For me, those issues were an economy that worked for as many people as possible instead of one where the wealth gap grew wider and wider; an effective healthcare system that all could afford; a way to rescue God's crumbling earth; an education system that worked for the marginalized student as much as the affluent one; and a society where everyone was welcomed, treated, and loved the same no matter what race, culture, language, sex, or income level.

To some I spoke with, those issues seemed to be difficult to fix. And yes, the devil is always in the details. But at some point, we have to realize that Christ's teachings are dead-on with these issues. To ignore them or have them become self-serving, blows up any of the bridges we need to build to understand and care for each other better.

Some pro-life advocates will say I left out the most important one—the right to life from the moment of conception. I don't take that lightly. The topic is worth more than a sentence or two. It can be very complicated—particularly when many pro-life advocates refuse to include or support from womb-to-tomb issues that take millions of lives, many of which I cite in "Storms and Pollution." We can't have it both ways.

Some people call it politics. I call it simply following what the scriptures teach us.

# 2042

**For some reason, this is the year that scares the living** hell out of many Americans.

It is the year projections indicate that white Americans will fall below 50 percent of the nation's population[9]. Minorities will no longer be the minority. People of color will out-number white Americans.

I hope I live to see that.

Why? Two reasons.

First, this scenario was the guiding principle of how and why America was founded. A refuge for anyone. "All men are created equal," the Declaration of Independence staunchly vows. Unfortunately, that which was declared was far from reality as European settlers killed and treated the indigenous Native American population and Black slaves with savagery and little regard for life let alone equality.

The inscription on the Statue of Liberty welcomes "the tired, the poor, those yearning to be free"...although freedom was really only meant for a certain caste. Pulitzer Prize winning author Isabel Wilkerson in her best-selling book *Caste* reveals that even Eastern and Southern Europeans were disregarded as less, but because they were white, their status became elevated.

Four hundred years after the first landing of slaves on American shores, many White Americans still fear the inability to be in control... to not be the ruling majority.

And while students throughout America pledge allegiance to the flag and state that we are "one nation under God, indivisible with liberty and justice for all," we are anything but.

Well-known political figure Pat Buchanan turned pundit once pontificated:

"America is headed, seemingly inexorably, to a future where a majority in this country traces its ancestors to Asia, Africa and Latin America, a future where this already fractured nation is even more multiracial, multiethnic, multilingual and multicultural than today." [10]

He was not happy about that.

Second, and perhaps more important than the rhetoric that was laid out by our founding fathers, is that of the scriptures. One cannot read the Good Book from cover to cover without understanding that God created one race and only one race—the human race. Oh sure, we see a variety of cultures and skin tones that developed over the centuries, but it is very clear that "there is no partiality with Him" (Eph. 6:9). And how disconcerting is it for the white populace to grasp or even admit that Jesus was a POC?

That "no partiality" truth, unfortunately, has not eliminated the fear many white Christians have toward that projected transition from majority to minority. Let's play a game of hypotheticals.

There is a church of 400. The congregation is overwhelmingly white. Over the next decade that church sees incredible growth. The Lord is working in unfathomable ways. The membership grows to 1,000. There is one interesting occurrence, however. Five hundred fifty of those new members are people of color. They are now in the majority.

How many of those original 400 white members do you believe would still be worshipping there? How many do you think would have sought another church in order to be around "people with whom I have more in common?"

Sadly, I think we know the answer to that question.

Why are so many white people afraid to be in the minority? Why do we feel uncomfortable being in the minority? Why are we the first ones to leave a gathering in which we are in the minority? Why do we feel that we have to remain in the majority to feel that everything is all right? Or as it should be?

That certainly wasn't how our founding fathers described "the land of opportunity" as veiled as those words might have been. And it certainly wasn't how God created man and his desired obedience to Him.

My wife loves her job. The other day she came home with a photo taken at her office of her team. Seven of them. Asians. Mid-Easterners. Blacks. And one white person. My wife. She loves her co-workers. She tells stories constantly about their families, their customs, their foods, their habits, their dialects, their sense of humor, their educational pursuits. The commonalities they all have as they walk through life. It's been a learning experience for her, but one that has perhaps been the most revealing and rewarding of her career.

Rewards.

I'm thinking that God may have a sly smile on his face come 2042 because we're going to have to figure out the rewards of all races working as One.

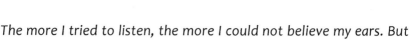

*The more I tried to listen, the more I could not believe my ears. But I'd better. Because there it was. And it was not an undercurrent. Oh sure. A lot of people didn't want to admit they felt this way. But their subtle comments with innuendo and actions revealed their true self. And more than I anticipated, it was outwardly overt. When a leading pundit like Patrick Buchanan holds nothing back and outwardly claims how disastrous it would be for minorities to become the majority in the US, it becomes a sad day indeed. Not only is that overtly racist (believing that Whites know best how to rule and are entitled to it because of their race), but it refutes everything Christ teaches in the New Testament. (New American Standard, Gal. 3.28, Rom. 2.11, Eph. 2.14, Eph. 6.9, 1 Cor. 12.13). I truly believe that much of the social and racial adversity that exits and laws surrounding it, will begin to dissipate once America's great melting pot truly melts more colors into the whiteness.*

# Politics and Religion

**As I was thinking about what to entitle this thought, I** wanted to come up with something really catchy that would pull everyone in the instant they saw it. That list of titles got very long and suffered severely from over-thinking.

So, I went back to the KISS principle—Keep It Simple, Stupid— realizing that perhaps no two words next to each other evoke such emotion, passion and spectrum-stretching opinions as—drum roll, please—POLITICS & RELIGION.

Some people will tell you that the two don't mix or shouldn't mix. After all, the Constitution of this very United States calls for a separation of church and state, so end of discussion. Except that opens a whole new kettle of fish when it comes to taxation, subsidies, education, freedom of speech, healthcare, etc., etc., etc. We're not going to go there, at least not now.

Then there are others who believe that their faith (and thus their morality) compels them to be involved in politics as nothing (unfortunately) impacts society more than the laws and policies of the government, which the last time I looked just happens to be governed by two different political parties with different platforms. And anything that affects society, some argue, affects morality and since morality is tied to religion (although more arguments to be made there later), one can't separate religion and politics.

Then there are others whose faith compels them to stay away from politics. They reason that if we all follow the Creator's guidelines, we understand that He is in control. So long as we follow Him there is no need to worry about what faction is deciding what for society.

Another group is the political animals that claim religion and faith should have nothing to do with how society and the economy operate. Let's just get some rules and laws in place that work best for the majority (meaning what *they* believe and want) and with the fine tuning of intelligence and science, we can make this a pretty livable society.

So, what do I believe? Now, you may expect me to stay clear of any one predisposition over another. After all, haven't I said that these posts are intended to reveal many different ways of thinking with the purpose of making readers contemplate their *thoughts for everyday living* just a little harder? Well, yes. But as you will see over time, sometimes I will choose sides with the intent for you to do just that—think about the position I have taken.

I weigh in with the second mode of thinking—one's faith compelling one to be involved in politics. Kind of. With a bit of a twist. For more on that twist, check out "The 70 Percent Club."

*This one is always a powder keg. Particularly during election years. What's crazy is that black churches preach one thing. White churches preach other things. And they often differ dramatically when proselytizing about how Christ intends us to scripturally view society's woes. Yes, Blacks tend to be more progressive. White congregations lean conservative. So what gives? Both worship the same God and Savior. So why the differences? Many books have been written. I don't intend to start another one here.*

*But I do believe that our Christian beliefs and mores should figure very strongly into our voting habits. I just question how accurately or sincerely some Christians want to learn the pain of the marginalized, seeking instead the path of the Pharisees. To me, one can't separate politics and religion. I just pray that more people would understand and study both politics and the scriptures better in order to be truly capable of making heart-felt intelligent decisions.*

# The 70 Percent Club

**Yeah. I know. I certainly decided to go bold with my prior** thought about Politics and Religion. But you know what they say, "Go Bold or Go Home."

Actually, the effort here isn't intended to be polarizing but rather unifying. At a time when media seem to spend a lot of time reporting the extremes (ok, I get that and actually understand it), I remain firmly affixed to the belief that not only are many of us guided by faith, but that most of us politically are not extremists. I guess about 70 percent of us fall just a bit right or left of center. The other 30 percent admittedly lean pretty far to the left or right in relatively equal proportions. They get way too much attention.

I read a lot. I always have. Perhaps that's because my grandmother, who lived next door to me when I grew up, was a schoolteacher. She always said reading was the most important subject. I still agree. It not only teaches, it helps develop one's communication skills.

I read about three hours a day—news, fiction, biographies, inspirational – about anything other than how-to and fix-it manuals. Not my forte. Ask my wife. Plus, the people who write those manuals could use a course or two in layman's language. But then again, I realize that those fixer-upper, techie types use a different part of their brain, so they get a pass. God made handymen for a reason.

What specifically I read is important though. I think this is where a lot of people, particularly those extreme 30-percenters, get it wrong. When you read, consider the source. Please. Particularly when it comes to politics and religion. There are some disturbing extremists out there. And in this age of social media, some of the sources I see people reposting and adhering to are, to use as polite a word as I can, bogus.

For instance, I have a friend who throws all sorts of stuff up on his social media pages trying to justify his political stance. Many of those posts' origins, when I track them, come from organizations that can't be traced. Outwardly illegitimate. Often identified as a bot. We all know where most of those come from—people who don't want to be identified because for whatever nefarious reason, they are up to no good spreading untruths.

So, here's my advice. Look to non-partisan outlets. For accurate data impacting the political arena, I suggest information provided by the likes of Pew Research, the Bureau of U.S. Statistics, the Government Accountability Office (GAO), Congressional Budget Office (CBO), the Brookings Institute. There are others. But if something strikes you as too off-center, it probably is. Research the source.

And don't go picking on the mainstream media. Yes, some *lean* a bit right, a bit left, but in large, journalists who make it to the top of the food chain have worked incredibly difficult, long hours with hard-fought verifiable research to back their stories. As a barometer, check out organizations who've won Pulitzers and other legitimate industry awards. Listen to them.

Okay. Let's switch for a minute to religion.

As a Christian, I am told to love my neighbor as myself and to love God with all my heart. It is He is who provides and directs our love. If I can do that, a lot of my prejudices and biases disappear. Or they should, even though no one is even close to perfection...and we must continually seek and confess.

America, perhaps more than any other country in the world, is a country of diverse religions and faiths. It is what makes us great. Most followers of those faiths and religions seek to make this country and this world a better place. We can all learn from each other. We should all love and want to help each other, even others with different theological backgrounds.

The problems of society are many. I think if we all began to list them and discuss them, we'd find that while we have some differences of opinion, those differences are more marginal and solvable than the certain select media that caters to the 30 percent wants us to think. Freedom of worship, a clean environment, a healthy economy, a strong education system, equality for everyone, healthcare for all, help for the needy, a fair judicial system, a giving society. Yes, the devil is in the details. But I suspect if we all sat in a room, we'd see that our differences politically and theologically aren't all that far apart and that we could indeed reach a more equitable consensus than what currently prevails.

Let's hear it for the 70 Percent Club!

*There are some days when I absolutely feel that most of us are on the same page. And then there are others when I don't. There is a plethora of examples, but let's take the gorilla in the room. COVID-19. It changed our world. In many ways, our brains. Both figuratively and literally. Not only did it kill more than five million people worldwide, but I think it might have fried many people's brains—both those who got it and survived, and those who refused to believe it was the great peril that all the top scientists in the world claimed. Some among the fried brains, well-educated. Well, at least we thought their educations were worth something. Maybe not. With little warning and far less reason, vast numbers of smart, intelligent, well-educated people were calling the pandemic a hoax. Ok, as well as some of the not-so-well-educated who couldn't put an intelligent sentence together if you spotted them the subject and verb. Whether the topic was vaccinations, masks or voodoo remedies, I sometimes began to think that the "Invasion of the Body Snatchers" had actually occurred. Difference of opinion is what makes the world go 'round and stimulates good conversation and innovation. But the "fringies" seem to be eating into too much of their share sometimes. Or at least getting far too much recognition.*

# The New Economy

**A few months into the pandemic there was a lot of talk** (and rightly so) about how science was having to find new ways to attack the coronavirus. But I wondered why there was not more discussion about how to attack and even change the economic paradigm. Look, we all wanted things to get back to normal socially and economically, but what if it was not possible, I wondered? Some said, "well that's not an acceptable question because we 'have to' otherwise, we will face economic ruin and devastation."

That answer presumes "well, that's the way we've always done it (the way the economy has always operated successfully), so that's what we have to do again." I've always hated that "well, we've always done it that way" response from my staff and colleagues. Think of the lack of innovation if we always adhered to that mentality.

So, what am I getting at?

Is there the need to work on a new economic model that works and can be successful under the new normal we may be facing? I'm thinking some really bright economists and entrepreneurs—equally as smart as those scientists in the medical field—could and should be working on how a successful new normal economy could not only operate but thrive. We seem to be too fixated on getting back to our cushy old business and social practices, when perhaps we should be thinking are there new and better ways to do business that this crisis is teaching us?

A few months into the pandemic, everyone seemed to be panicking about the economy. The mantra became: "We have to save the economy. We have to get back to normal. We'll be ruined if we can't return to normalcy, both economically and socially." As circumstances drew more dire, businesses changed. Yes, some went under. But many learned not only how to survive but thrive. Doing things differently. That some things were better. Things that never would have been instituted unless forced to do so. Economic experts looked into their crystal balls and declared a new booming economy around the corner. Let's hope we've learned enough about the New Economy to prove them correct.

# Bridge the Gap

**Just down the street from where I live is a wonderful** church. When I say down the street, I literally mean a 90-second drive or a five-minute walk. Nearby, within a mile, there are three other churches. Many of the parishioners actually do walk. That's the great part about living in a walking community.

But over the course of many months, I noticed something. That church down the street was a Black church. The others were White churches. And I'm not referring to the exterior hue of each building.

Martin Luther King, Jr. once said that the most segregated hour of the week was Sunday morning between 11 and 12 o'clock.

If all these churches worship the same God, then why the separation? Why the segregation? I'm sure if you spoke to the pastors, and perhaps a handful of church members, they would tell you that they are open to all creeds, colors and cultures. And they are. Mostly. But for some reason, diversity is not catching on in most churches these days.

Some claim that it is a matter of comfort. What's always been. Others claim that it is definitely political. Eighty one percent of White evangelicals voted for Donald Trump and claim to be solidly Republican. Ninety percent of Blacks voted for Joe Biden, many of them hardcore "believers."

So, what gives?

What do the scriptures say about social issues? Justice? Evil? Right from wrong? Forgiveness? Caring for the least of these? Greed? Capitalism? Socialism? Democracy?

The dirty little secret that most churches won't admit, is that social issues—not faith issues—often drive its parishioners' actions.

Black congregations are a bit more open to that admission. Suffering and thorns and redemption are key New Testament messages that most Black churches embrace.

The white evangelical church often charges forward embracing Old Testament themes of authoritarianism, paternalism, nationalism and out-right John Wayne induced machoism. Easy to see why nary the twain of the Black and White church shall meet.

But in this community, there is hope. Two of the churches—one Black, one White—only a mile separating each other, realized there was a problem. They needed to talk. So, they did. A group of 12 "disciples" formed, six White and six Black, and began meeting regularly to talk about their lives, the issues challenging them daily and how the scriptures should guide them through the various terrains.

They were trying to bridge the gap. It wasn't easy at first. Admittedly, there were prejudices, misconceptions, and outright erroneous awareness. But as they talked and studied the gospel, they began to grow closer. They began to understand. And cherish. And love each other as brothers.

In addition to a new-found spiritual bond, they began socializing with each other—even if it meant they were the only minority in the room on occasion. That discomfort had subsided. Under God, we are all the same no matter the idiosyncrasies and social circumstances that the world might throw at us or want us to hold far too firmly.

Bridge the Gap. What a great concept!

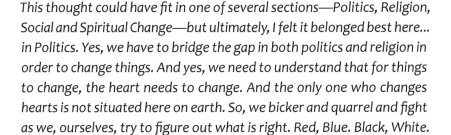

*This thought could have fit in one of several sections—Politics, Religion, Social and Spiritual Change—but ultimately, I felt it belonged best here... in Politics. Yes, we have to bridge the gap in both politics and religion in order to change things. And yes, we need to understand that for things to change, the heart needs to change. And the only one who changes hearts is not situated here on earth. So, we bicker and quarrel and fight as we, ourselves, try to figure out what is right. Red, Blue. Black, White. We are nowhere near figuring it out. When, as the data bears out, the*

White part of the Christian church votes one way and the Black part of the Christian church votes another way, there is serious division. But it does not have to remain that way. It cannot remain that way. While both sides seek a revelation, we hesitate to understand that Revelation comes closer to fruition with each setting of the sun.

Discussion is always good. Some people hate to discuss anything. That's because after a few exchanges, it becomes apparent that they really don't know their subject matter. They become embarrassed that they cannot logically and factually support their position. So, they raise their voices and stomp off waiving their hands, muttering to themselves.

Case in point. Have you ever sat down with an adversary to discuss a situation on which you had opposing views? After all the back-and-forth he slaps himself on his head and utters, "Oh, my gosh, you're right. I can't believe I've been so stupid and unenlightened for so many years. I will now change my point of view to yours."

Never. Which is why I tip my hat to those six Black and White brothers who at least were prepared to go down a very uncomfortable road to have some of those discussions. At the end of the day, no one killed anyone. They learned a lot about each other. They even came to see things in ways they hadn't perceived before. The gap began to close. That's a start.

# One Race: Walk the Walk

**One Friday not too long ago, I marched. I marched** against racial and social injustice with a faith-based group. Reportedly, there were 15,000 of us. Two others were Walter and Helen.

I bumped almost literally into Walter and Helen while marching to the state capitol. Walter was in a wheelchair. He was apparently suffering from some sort of neurological disorder. His wife, Helen, was pushing him. Both were in the 70's. Both were White.

I couldn't help but ask them. Why are you doing this?

Don't you know you might get hurt? Don't you know you could catch the corona virus? Don't you know it's freakin' hot out here!

They didn't care. Their hearts were hurting. They remembered the 1960s very well. They remembered 1968. Martin Luther King, Jr. Robert F. Kennedy. The riots. The burning cities. The protests at the Democratic National Convention in Chicago. The election of Richard Nixon.

"We saw the unrest, saw the passion for progress, saw people willing to die for equality and freedom. But somewhere along the way, many of us became complacent. We patted ourselves on the back for shining moments when our Black brothers and sisters gained some acclaim in business or entertainment or government and thought, 'My, my, aren't we making progress?' But it was token progress. We need real progress, and we need God to change hearts. That's why we're here. We think this time is different. It has to be."

My eyes got wet. I told them how much I appreciated them.

Neither their message nor actions were lost on me. As frail as Walter and Helen were, they were there to walk the walk. No more simply agreeing that things weren't equal and needed to change. No more simply going to church, professing Christian beliefs, and loyally tithing only to go home to the comforts of the well-manicured, affluent neighborhood and expensive cars in the driveway. Walter and Helen decided to walk the walk – even at their age – no matter how *difficult* and *uncomfortable*. It was important to them. Incredibly important.

If Walter and Helen can walk the walk, can't we?

———————◇———————

*Whenever I go to one of these rallies or marches, I tend to look around and see where I fall on the age spectrum. Gratefully, new younger blood has picked up the mantel to fight wrongs and injustice. Otherwise, the marches would take twice as long. And may need to be called "crawls." It brings back remembrances of that era. But here I was, trying to be super careful. The pandemic was raging. But Black and Brown brothers were being murdered in the streets by those who they thought were there to take care of them. Provide their safety. And people were mad. Because it kept happening over and over. The group of 15,000 marching that day was organized by a faith-based organization, One Race Movement. Music rocked the crowd. Speakers talked boldly of Christ's message of justice, reconciliation, and oneness. It was important to Walter and Helen not to lose sight of Christ's message—that oneness and reconciliation with our brothers of all colors and cultures. That's the way He would have wanted it. That's what He preached.*

# Civil

*"In my life, I have done all I can to demonstrate that the way of peace, the way of love and non-violence is the more excellent way. Now it is your turn to let freedom ring."*

- Congressman John Lewis

**Did you ever wonder why or how the civil rights move-**ment got named? Afterall, it could have been called the human rights movement or equal rights or Black rights or social equality rights. But it wasn't. It was called *civil* rights.

If you go to your thesaurus, you will see words such as polite, courteous, well-mannered, well-bred, gracious, respectful, gallant, cultured, civilized, decent, mannerly listed as synonyms for *civil*.

Martin Luther King, Jr. and his brave colleagues were taught civility by their parents...who had been taught by their parents...who had been taught by their parents...and so on, all the way back to the Civil War which was anything but. Ironic? Certainly.

What the founders of the civil rights movement understood was that change was not going to be easy. Probably anything but civil. It would be difficult. It would be dangerous. It would take time. Yet violence and raising arms would only demonstrate hate to combat hate.

Hardly a formula for civil results.

What would begin to work...over time...would be a gallant, civilized, disciplined approach toward the goal of decency and equality for all races.

It was important—no, vital—that the early demonstrators remain civil while beatings and hate manifested itself upon them.

It is not ironic that most of those brave men and women were people of faith, following God's teachings. And it was exactly those teachings of fairness, compassion, equity, and justice to which they adhered, that would begin to create a seismic shift in America's culture.

The civil rights movement of Martin Luther King, Jr. is now 60-plus years old. Much has been achieved, but there are so many more bridges to cross.

Some will argue that racism has diminished over time. Others disagree. They point to inequality in education, career opportunities, finances, and even the way one of color is silently and subconsciously judged—notably even by the police.

Some question whether the civility of the early-era civil rights movement works today.

John Lewis thought so as he passed the mantle to let freedom ring.

While the protests of the 60's are legendary, chronicled and driven by television, which was the new medium of that time, today's protests are different. They now are chronicled by today's new medium of social media, however one wishes to define that. It is a medium used way too often by the misinformed, narrow-minded and cowardly.

Opinions may be anything but civil. But protests must remain so... while still having bite.

Racism has stared White America in the face for decades. We've learned. We've advanced. We've become more tolerant. But is it good enough simply to claim that we are not racist? Yes, we've seen and learned what racism is and what it has done to our society. We may even like to claim that we treat everyone the same and that all lives matter. But do we really? Do they really? Do Black Lives Matter? Can you even utter that phrase?

We must take the next step. We must learn to be anti-racist. We must raise our voice. We must cross the bridge. Along the way, we must be gracious, respectful, decent, courageous, and brave—admitting that many of us don't know what we don't know.

Be civil as we continue to confront and fight racism. Civil disobedience. It's a good thing. Ask John Lewis.

*Looking back at film and into my memories, it amazes me to this day that those involved in the early civil rights movement not only preached non-violence, but lived it. Time and time again, they were beaten, brutalized, bandaged, hospitalized and even killed. Yet, they marched on realizing that anything less than civil would be a detriment to the cause. I could not have done it. I would have cracked. Especially if someone had gone after my best friend, or sister, or daughter or wife. But to fight back would have simply turned the vernacular to "see what these savages are all about ..." Theirs was truly the Jesus tale of turning the other cheek. Many of these crusaders came out of a church-inspired upbringing which led John Lewis, MLK, Jr. and others to create the Beloved Community, knowing that without their humility, that peace and harmony would never been attainable. It still has a way to go. But thank God for those early civil leaders.*

# Mad or Sad

**We humans are an emotional bunch. It is the one charac-**teristic that God gave us that distinguishes us from the rest of the earth's species. Things pull on our heart. We exude emotion.

We experience joy, sorrow, love, hate, fear, and bravery. We get mad and we are sad.

I get mad sometimes when I hear someone say or do something that is totally stupid, ignorant, wrong or downright dangerous. I can't tell you how many times I've stared incredulously at the TV in recent months as people spew hate against other races, berate those wearing (or not wearing) facial masks, or stand for careless acts against the environment. I could go on and on. I'm sure you could, too.

Recently, an on-air commentator responded to a social media post by a U.S. Senator with a post of his own. It said "F#&% you." Excuse me? Okay, so you don't agree with his position. But expletive deleted. Really?! What ensued? Thousands and thousands of additional angry posts taking one side or another. Really accomplished a lot. Not!

Another recent event had a flight attendant assaulted and injured by a passenger simply because she asked him to wear a face mask in consideration of other passengers. Assaulted! Injured! Really!?

I get mad when I hear about these things, sometimes really mad. Demonstrably so. But when I do, am I really responding any better than those who performed the original act? I quickly, or sometimes not-so-quickly, move from mad to sad, realizing that there are a lot of people who just really don't comprehend wrong and perhaps never will. Sad.

Proverbs (14:29) tells us "He who is slow to anger has great understanding, but he who is quick tempered exalts folly." Okay. Okay. Okay. Breathe. Try to understand where these angry people are coming from. While I genuinely may never agree with the angry or despicable act, should I not ask or try to understand what in this person's life has brought him or her to that point. Should I not actually show a little compassion?

Man, that's a hard one.

People don't just blow or draw dreadful conclusions without the prompting of some deep-seated shortcoming in their lives. Losses. Perceived acts of unfairness. Too much career or family pressure. Relationships gone bad. Health issues. And sometimes, unfortunately, an early life environment with shortcomings that totally don't prepare a person for the realities of daily living and loving.

The New Testament encourages us to put aside anger, wrath, malice, slander and abusive speech. Be quick to hear, slow to speak and slow to anger.[11]

I don't know about you, but I need to work on that. When someone takes the opposite position of what I believe is right, I sometimes get angry. My voice often raises. My gestures become more animated. That's wrong. I need to take a breath.

Will challenging or screaming at the other person (or TV screen) really make things better? Will that person instantly say, "Gosh, I'm really glad you've screamed at me and shared your position, because it's all clear to me now and I truly understand. Thank you so very much for your angry response. It was so helpful for me to understand what you called 'my stupidity.'?"

Ok, you say. But what if that person's perspective is truly wrong and harmful. Paul's letter to the Ephesians indicates that we should "speak truth" to our neighbor and even "be angry" but "not to sin."[12]

There is a way to do that. I'm still trying to learn.

*An angry man stirs up strife and a hot-tempered man abounds in transgressions (Prov. 29:22).*

I need to work on yelling at that TV, I guess.

*I've found it difficult to stand by and watch wrong after wrong, injustice after injustice, and not get mad. Yes, I should try to understand. Perhaps if I had walked or been raised in the perpetrator's shoes, I'd feel differently. I hope, however, that I would never fail to be able to identify actual wrong or sinful behavior for what it is. Okay. Okay. There are certainly gray areas. Lying is a sin. But if you are housing Jews in Germany in the 40's and the Gestapo comes by to ask if you are harboring Jews, you lie. Because it's for the greater good of mankind. The problem now is that the greater good has become all too twisted in many minds. So, I get angry. It really shouldn't be that difficult. But it is. If people would simply read the four gospels—or even just the words in red, depicting Jesus' revelations and instructions, what a better place this would be. So, if you really want to make America great again, read Matthew through John. That would be a good start.*

# The Taj Mahal It Ain't

**At one point in my career, I worked for a professional** sports team. On game day, my boss and I were usually the first ones at the stadium other than the grounds crew and operations staff. Yes, early.

It was a great gig even though the stadium was a long drive from our training facility (and homes). But each gameday weekend, Charlie and I would pull into our designated parking spots under the stadium (how do you say "perk"?) to begin prep for the long fourteen-hour day ahead—one in which we would presumably or hopefully come away with a "W."

The facility was city-owned, so we had little control over way too many operational elements. We wanted to have the stadium appear as first class as possible to VIP dignitaries and media. We wanted our city and franchise to reflect well to visitors.

Consequently, we would do our best to encourage, coddle, and outright cajole the head of operations to make the facility look, well... first class. Or at least have some semblance of cleanliness.

The season opener arrived. As we pulled underneath the stadium to our designated parking, we passed the locker rooms, media elevator, VIP entrance, concessions compound and worker check-in. The entire route to our parking spots was a mess.

As we were unloading our cars with the tools for the day's demands, the head of operations rode up on a golf cart welcomingly, waving, and smiling.

"Big day, eh?" he effused.

"Yes, it sure is," responded my boss. "But, hey John, do you think you could get your guys to give a little more attention to cleaning up down here. It looks a fright, and that's not exactly the type of impression we want to make to our out-of-town guests."

"Gosh, I'm so sorry," came the reply. "Show me a few things you are talking about so I can be sure to point them out and have them taken care of."

Charlie hopped on the golf cart. As they rode through the facility's catacombs, my boss pointed out as pleasantly as possible, some of the areas that needed attention.

"No problem. We'll take care of it," was the response. "And I'm really sorry, but I assure you this place will look like the Taj Mahal by next game."

My boss smiled, thanked him...then proceeded to put in the fourteen-hour day that ended with a shellacking.

The next gameday arrived. Again, we pulled into the stadium's underbelly early. My boss looked around.

"What in the world! They haven't done a thing. This place looks just as bad as the last game."

He didn't even bother unloading. He called John on the hotline phone attached to the wall.

"John, I just pulled in. Can you come over here?"

There was a bit of annoyance in his voice. John zoomed up moments later in his golf cart.

"Hey, Charlie. How ya' doing this morning? Another big game, eh? What can I do for ya?"

"John, you told me that you'd have this place all cleaned up. 'Looking like the Taj Mahal,' I believe were your words. It doesn't look like you've done anything. Look at that over there. That's a mess."

John appeared stunned, not to mention a bit hurt.

"Charlie, we did clean up. I oversaw that area myself. It's clean."

Charlie didn't know what to say. To him, it was dirty. To John, it was clean.

I said not a word but realized there was a moral in this story. Some people, no matter how long they look at something, can't see the errors in what they are seeing—or thinking. Why is that? Is it a cultural thing? Education or lack thereof? A pre-ingrained notion from childhood? A learned behavior from an uneducated or prejudicial source? A bad experience perhaps?

Obviously, the subject in question is clearly dirty. Why can't they see that?

Or perhaps it's a bit less clear. To us, it's dirty. To them, it is not. Is it merely perspective? Or is it the recognition that one is willing to consider some data and consciously deem it more important than other data? Which data is correct? Who is right?

There is a deep lessen here, I think. Sometimes, one perspective is clearly dead-laser on. Sometimes, it isn't.

So, let's talk about it. We don't seem to do enough of that these days.

To this day, I find this hard to explain. How can two people look at exactly the same situation and see it entirely differently. Is it upbringing? The way they were taught? What and how they were exposed to various aspects of life? An experience or trauma at some time during their lives? A chemical imbalance? A cross-wired brain? A neuron mix-up? A brain-washing at some juncture? How do some justify killing (war, capital punishment) while others can't justify it or at least tread a line somewhere in-between? Why does one cry "freedom of choice" not to wear a mask or get vaccinated (evidently not too concerned about the 5 million who have died due to the refusal of cautions that drastically reduce deaths), while at the same time protest and rail against "freedom of choice" for reproductive rights. Why is one freedom of choice that results in death okay, while the other is not? Not taking sides. Just asking the question. Trying to understand the rationale. Trying to understand what one person sees and the other doesn't. Surely the sky is blue. Even when it may have more of a gray tint. What's your preference? Can we at least talk about it?

# The 100 MPH Fastball

**The baseball scout was insistent.**

"This right-hander throws harder than anyone I've ever seen. I've clocked him well over 100 miles per hour. I guarantee you that he will be the savior of our franchise," he told the team's hierarchy, fans, media and anyone else who would listen.

Soon everyone was checking out the right-hander. He was drafted number one, signed for a significant bonus and sent right to the big leagues. He wore uniform number forty-five. Sure, he was unseasoned. But, man did he have a great fastball!

All was not what it seemed, however. He had control problems. He walked more than he struck out. He hit a lot of batters. He groused at the umpires and sometimes even his catchers. He sometimes pouted boisterously. He felt he could set his own rules. He was not a team player. He was cancer in the locker room. He didn't understand the basics of the game. And he didn't want to listen to coaching from seasoned veterans and coaches who had been there before. It was all about him.

Okay. He had a couple of good outings. Just enough so the team stuck with him and stood by him. But savior he wasn't. As those around him got sucked in and sucked down to his level, the team began to flounder. There was unrest.

Pretty soon, both fans and hierarchy began to understand the severity of Number 45's flaws. While there was one thing they really liked, the rest was an abomination.

I wonder if we sometimes don't treat Christianity and politics in much the same way. We overlook a lot of what we consider "little sins" because someone is so good at championing against the "big sins" without understanding that there is no such thing as a little sin and a big sin in God's eyes.

And in the world of politics, we all too often make one cause more important than other critical ones simply because we want to believe that the 100-mph fastball outweighs everything else.

———————✕———————

*Correct. An allegory.*

# The Land of Oosa

**Once upon a time there was a country called Oosa. It was** founded by explorers from a foreign land. Many, many miles across the seas.

Those who discovered the new land were relieved. The voyage had not been easy. The ships had battled violent storms. Mountainous waves. Blistering heat. And time. They were sailing to the unknown.

Many of their countrymen feared they would sail off the edge of the earth into oblivion and a great fire. But they didn't.

One bleary-eyed morning, a shout rang out.

"Ahoy! Land! Land! I see land!"

Indeed.

As the battered ships slipped slowly onto the new earth, there were shouts of joy. Relief. Gratitude. Although the land was strange, it would become their land. They found it. They embraced it. It was theirs.

Soon, strange beings began to peer through the trees. They weren't like the new seafarers. They had reddish skin and dressed in animal clothes, feathers and sometime wore paint on their faces. The new settlers wanted to learn more about these wildmen. Were they friendly? Were they evil? Could the two groups co-exist?

The settlers told the Redmen that they had named their new land Oosa, a word from their foreign world that meant "united." The Redmen taught the men from Oosa how to hunt and fish and even till the new land. The Oosa men were not used to the climate. Many had become weak and ill on the voyage. Many did not survive the first several months.

They needed help—more help than they felt the Redmen could provide.

Others like them came from across the waters. Soon, the Oosans were bringing dark-skinned men and women from worlds unknown to help them hunt and fish and till the fields. The Redmen found the dark-skinned creatures unusual but tried to help.

Over the years, more and more Oosa men and women arrived. They used a word called "freedom" as they began to build a new life on this new earth. They patted each other on the back, creating villages and trading posts unlike those to which the Redmen were accustomed.

They began to steal the Redmen's land and battled them to death with their superior weapons unless they submitted. Or left. They forced the dark-skinned creatures to clear the newly claimed land and to work the businesses they created.

Eventually, Oosa spread for mile after mile along its new coastline. Farms called plantations grew what the Redmen had shown their alleged new friends would thrive. The Redmen were pushed further and further from their native land, a land now tilled by the dark faces brought in and forced to propagate by the Oosa tribe. Over the years, Oosa grew larger and larger.

Several hundred years passed. Those of Oosa created schools, banks, industries large and small and churches. Rules were written to govern and regulate those social and economic necessities. The Redmen and those of dark skin were not consulted.

Eventually, those not of the Oosa tribe spoke up. The rules were stacked against them. The rules did not take their needs and safety into consideration. The rules actually penalized them for not being like those who founded Oosa.

Those of Oosa were reminded that the very word meant "united" and that the soil was founded as Oosa men and women sought "freedom." But the Oosa world was anything but united and many citizens were anything but free.

The Oosans pushed back, explaining that it was they who founded this new world. They were happy to have those who didn't exactly look like them, but those non-Oosans had to understand that the rules were written with those Oosans in mind.

No sense pushing back. That's the way it was. Whether overtly written or etched between the lines. That's the way it was. That's the way it is.

---

*It's certainly not difficult to understand the allegorical tale of the land of Oosa. Even the name should be a giveaway. And while it's incredibly difficult to tell the tale in a few short paragraphs of how this country developed, there should be no mistake that in the land of Oosa there were a lot of mistakes. Most notably prejudice and racism. And they permeated every area of society—law, education, finance, industry and even the church. The result was violence at times and unfathomable naivety at others. That naivety has not dissipated. Many today, still believe and adhere to "white makes might" or "white makes right." Meanwhile, racial harmony gets more and more difficult as cultural diversity pervades society and the original Oosans wonder what's going to happen to them when and if they become a minority themselves. So, the system they put in place more than 400 years ago, fights to keep its unspoken traditions and rules in place, while pretending there was never really any favoritism at all. Not then. Not now. And we all know differently.*

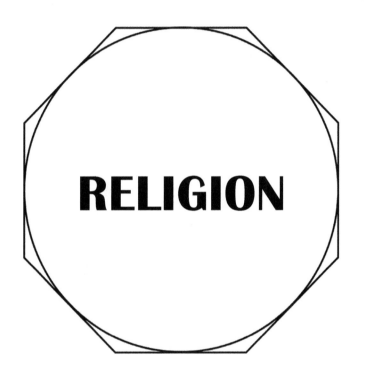

# RELIGION

# Dream

**Eddie had a dream the other night. Nothing new. Eddie** had lots of dreams. He only paid attention to those that made him happy or shook him to the point of taking action.

Like the time in his life he had this recurring dream. He was going blind. He knew he had not been to the eye doctor recently. He made an appointment. Result—he had an eye disease. He would be blind in a few years if he didn't begin treatment.

Whoa. Scary. Caught it just in time.

Another time, he kept having a dream about someone he'd wronged years ago. The dream would begin with him seeing this person from afar. He made every attempt to get to him. He wanted to apologize. Tell the person how grief-stricken he had been over the wrong. All these years. But he would always wake up before he could connect. One day, he decided he would find that person and call him. It took quite an effort to get a telephone number within their network of mutual friends and acquaintances. But finally, he did.

He called. Said hello. Exchanged pleasantries. There did not seem to be any malice on the other end. Eddie finally just blurted out the reason he was calling. There was a short pause on the other end.

"Eddie," said the voice, "don't worry about it. I forgave you long ago. I heard you had changed. I knew any resentment would eat me up. I chose not to live like that. Love you for calling."

The recurring dream went away.

But a new dream was really bothering him. In it, Eddie had died and was on his way to an afterlife. He was hoping it was heaven or whatever heaven was. After all, he had lived a pretty decent life. And he had apologized—eventually—for that major wrong. That had to be worth something.

But in the dream, he was handed three pieces of paper, each with a different checklist, as he ascended the golden stairway. At least the stairway was golden. That had to be a good sign.

He was told to present one checklist to the gatekeeper when he got there as only one would grant him access.

One list included all the things he'd done wrong in his life. All the boxes were checked. "Not good," thought Eddie. The second was broken down into Big Wrongs and Little Wrongs. Not many check marks in the big column, Eddie noticed and thought, "This one is better to present". The last listed all his life's wrongs, but no check marks.

"Man, this one must be wrong," thought Eddie. "Someone is trying to trick me into handing in this obviously false check list."

He arrived at the gate. The gatekeeper was radiant. Majestic. Eddie was prepared to hand him the second list and hope for the best. Before he could, the gatekeeper reached out and took the one with no checks.

Eddie was dumbfounded. And scared. Surely someone would figure out that he was anything but sinless during his time on earth.

He looked into the gatekeeper's eyes. He had never seen eyes like that before. Loving. So...forgiving. The gatekeeper took the other two lists and tore them in half.

"You won't need these," he smiled, keeping the unchecked list. "I've taken care of those for you."

Eddie fell to his knees. He got it. Unconditional love. Grace.

————————✕————————

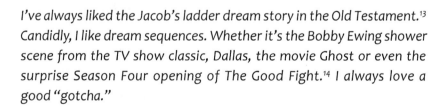

*I've always liked the Jacob's ladder dream story in the Old Testament.[13] Candidly, I like dream sequences. Whether it's the Bobby Ewing shower scene from the TV show classic, Dallas, the movie Ghost or even the surprise Season Four opening of The Good Fight.[14] I always love a good "gotcha."*

This one is a bit different. The first two examples are ones I personally lived through. The last, with the stairway to heaven...well, it's just something I believe an awful lot of people think about but never really admit. Particularly those who are not sure how all this will end.

I am sure. Faith and grace give me that. But I was trying to think of a good way to communicate that to so many who believe an afterlife is tied to how good or bad we are while living our earthly lives. We will never be good enough to enter heaven's gates based on our own merits. Thankfully, Christ took on all our wrongs on that cross and with his resurrection. It sounds rather simple. Maybe it is. But maybe it's not because it seems so unrealistic that anyone would or could do that for another. That's what makes him God and us not. That's what makes Christianity unique.

My biggest dilemma though was depicting how Eddie, who hadn't grasped that concept totally, was still going to get to go through the pearly gates without understanding that. Where was his profession of faith? I kept trying to find a way to include that without being too overt. I sometimes prefer the reader go between the lines to see how I got there. In this case, the person he calls provides that answer when he says, "I've heard you've changed." That's the clue that Eddie was a believer. But even believers sometimes find it hard to understand the concept of grace and still want to cling to that checklist. The message here is that you don't have to. It won't work. Grace.

# The Firepit

**All of us have things we gravitate to in times of chaos** and stress. Where do we go to break the monotony, chaos and stress that at times seem all around us?

Some put on a headset and escape with their favorite recording artist. Some workout or simply go for a quiet walk. Or perhaps the serenity of a chapel. Others open yet another bottle of wine.

We all need a respite from the craziness.

One of my life's little pleasures is the firepit. I recently moved. Downsized. And one of the things I miss is my firepit. I spent four years in California wine country, and the calm at the end of the week's storm was always the firepit overlooking the vineyards.

Back East and before the downsize, weather permitting, I often ended my week at the firepit on the back patio below the rear deck. It was awesome as the sun began to set and darkness edged in. Glass of wine in hand, I would sit there and just gaze into the fire for up to an hour trying to figure out what just happened that week.

I called it my DMM moment. Don't Mess with Me. My wife understood.

That fire was an interesting fire. As much as it provided heat and a bit of catharsis, I realized it could be dangerous. If I got too close, I got burned. Much like my thoughts of the week. Where had I been burned? Where was it okay to let situations simply burn themselves out or go up in flames? When was I to use that fire to light a fire in me, to cook a situation into something excellent and edible?

The dichotomy of that fire was not lost on me. Sometimes it provided much welcomed warmth and calm. Other times it could be debilitating.

I wondered about things I had said to people that week. Was I kind, helpful, gracious, understanding, and forgiving? Or was I irritable, irrational, unreasonable, and even despicable at times?

We've all heard things come out of a person's mouth and thought, "Not sure I would have said that if I were you." Perhaps we've even realized that about our own words at times.

The trouble is, once they are uttered, they can't be taken back. Oh sure. We can try. Apologies. "What I meant to say was...," but the damage had been done.

A friend in a really good marriage once told me, "My wife and I got into a pretty heated argument one night. We both said things we shouldn't have said. But when she uttered the 'D' word, I was taken aback. She later apologized. Said she didn't mean it. But I could never forget it. Our marriage was never quite the same after that."

The tongue. Such a small part of our body. Yet perhaps the part capable of inflicting the most lasting damage. Like the bit in a horse's mouth, the rudder of a ship, or a small spark that sets a forest ablaze, it has so much power.[15]

So, as I gaze into the firepit, I begin to understand that managing my words may be even more important than collecting my thoughts.

*The metaphor of a fire has been used over and over again. I've always found fires soothing. But then again, I've never had my house go up in flames, been in a fiery car wreck, been caught in a forest fire or been to hell. Although there was that weekend in Toledo. I've often sat quietly fireside and found it consoling - especially after a long week. I sometimes don't always like my reflections. Particularly those circumstances I didn't feel I could fix. At least readily. That's why in my illustration, I ventured down the path of the spoken word. Those little quips that we say in angst, despair, confusion even jest, often just don't fall well on the listener's ears. It's not only hard to take them back; it's impossible to take them back. I'm a big proponent of trying to clear my head before weekend time with my spouse begins. She doesn't deserve a lot of the*

*messed-up clutter and vengeance that's up there, particularly when she had nothing to do with it. Some weeks it's harder than others. Some weeks the fire has to burn a little longer.*

# Perception. Reality.

**"Do as I say, not as I do."**

We've all heard that expression. But what does it mean?

Does it imply that I know what to do but don't do it? Does it imply that I know right from wrong and can articulate it, but I still mess up?

Hmm. Interesting questions, huh? Here's someone's take. And he's a pretty famous guy, albeit a bit of a rebel.

> *The good I want to do, I don't practice. Instead, I practice the very evil that I don't want. But if I'm doing the very thing that I don't want, I am no longer the one doing it, but evil that dwells within me. (Romans 7: 19-20, NASB)*

As I shared this with a friend, he looked at me and said, "Man, that's messed up."

So, the discussion began. I admitted that I often do things I really don't want to do or know that I shouldn't do. I try to rationalize them away. Heat of the moment. Brain lapse. Epitome of frustration. A crime of passion. Well, not necessarily a crime, but you get the picture.

He began to come around. "Yep, happens to me all the time, too."

"So, do you sweep those moments under the rug," I asked, "or do you try to figure out what the heck happened and how to not let it happen again."

Another quizzical look.

"I guess it depends on what it was," he replied. "Some things are worse or bigger problems than other things."

I was starting to reel him in.

"So, we should worry more about fixing the big errors of our ways, and not worry too much about the little ones."

I phrased it as a statement, not a question.

"Yeah, I guess that's right," he answered. "Kinda like that book *Don't Sweat the Small Stuff.*"[16]

I continued to probe.

"So, I guess the goal then is to try to eliminate all the big stuff so we are left with just a bunch of little errors of our ways. I guess the government surely would run better if we could eliminate all the big problems in this country and whittle them down to the itty-bitty ones."

Yes. I was baiting him.

"Yeah, but that will never happen," he retorted. "Too many divisive and diverging viewpoints and deep-rooted, conflicting positions."

"So, who's right?" I asked.

He was stuck. I'm not sure he was ready to fix America's problems in this conversation.

"I have another question for you,"

"Fire away. Not sure I did all that well with that last one."

"Kinda the same topic. Do you think there are big sins and little sins?"

"Well, sure. Like, I mean murder, torture, adultery, pure hate and meanness are right up there. A little white lie, not so much."

I began to rattle off others: wickedness, greed, evil, envy, strife, deceit, malice, gossip, slander, hypocrisy, insolence, arrogance, boastfulness, disobedience, untrustworthy, unloving, unmerciful, hard-heartedness, and indifference.[17]

"Whoa. Whoa. Whoa! That's a heavy list."

"Yes, it is," I responded. "Pretty big burdens to carry. But you know, I'm probably guilty of many of those."

"Yeah, me too, I suppose. Guess I better not 'fess up to my wife, though. She might make me sleep on the couch or kick me out."

I had him right where I wanted him. My famous friend, the Apostle Paul, from the earlier quote, was about to explain how to never get kicked out ever again—no matter how big or little he perceived the errors of his ways.

Perception is not always reality.

————————⟡————————

*We have a distorted view of right and wrong. Most of us think that if we can simply diminish the tacky little things we do wrong ever so often, we'll be considered "good people." We're okay (in our minds) just so long as we don't screw up and do one of the "big, awful things"—or, especially, get caught doing one. After all, we have our reputations to think of. In our heads, we keep a score. Sometimes, we keep others' score too. That way if their score of wrongs is worse than ours, we can conclude we're doing okay. I mean no one is perfect, right? Well. Correct. When original wrong or sin (as uncomfortable as that term can be) came into the world, we were all doomed to a life of imperfection. And while we try to put wrongs into various-sized buckets like teeny, small, medium, large, gargantuan and deadly, reality is that in God's eyes, every wrong—every sin—is a sin. He doesn't put them into categories. Fortunately, He's provided a way in which that slate can be washed clean no matter how dirty. No other religion in the world offers that grace. The afterlife in other religions is determined by misdeeds or accomplishments. I choose Grace (Ephesians 2:8-9; Titus 3:5-7).*

# Red and Yellow, Black and White

**I was about to write about running and marriage again.** I changed my mind.

The events around America recently have altered things a bit. I don't know about you, but I'm having a hard time sleeping at night and concentrating during the day.

I'm kicking myself.

Growing up in an era when the civil rights movement came to the forefront, I was an advocate for justice and equality. How can one argue with justice and equality? It is a prolific message of the scriptures. That's how my parents raised me.

They would take me to church and we would sing, "Red and Yellow, Black and White. They are precious [equal] in His sight," says the song "Jesus Loves the Little Children." That pretty much says it all.

As I went off to college, started a career, and began my profession, I attempted to follow those mores and values...or at least thought I was. I was unbelievably moved when America elected its first Afro-American president. I watched that inauguration over lunch at a bar in small-town America, shoulder to shoulder with a Black man who had pulled in off the interstate just to watch it as well. As he left the bar to go on his way, we hugged. It was one of life's poignant moments.

But then something happened. While I was pretending that racial and social and economic injustice was waning, the lion broke through my invisible barriers and began to roar. I had not been paying attention.

Sure, I was outraged when Black men and women were unjustifiably abused, arrested, harassed and even murdered. And I could quote the statistics of education, income and healthcare disparity between those of color and those of non-color. Good for me.

Non-color. An interesting term, you think. But think of that term as a synonym for invisible. Because that's where much of America has been—invisible—as so little has really changed since the civil rights movement of the 60's. Fifty-plus years ago!

I read an interesting column during the height of the pandemic in 2020. It talked about how we don't need sports right now. "Wow," I thought at first, "That's a different take on everything else we've been hearing—about how sport is the great healer, how it brings us all together." The point of the article was, if we had sports to watch and consume, we (including many athletes) would be distracted and not concentrating on or paying attention to the full face of justified unrest (because many, certainly would not care to or be too busy).

People are mad. Rightly so. But I think God is mad, too. Thankfully, He is in control. Like it or not, understand it or not, God is always in control. God has a plan. I think it's more than reasonable to believe that God is not happy because we have turned our hearts and eyes from standing side-by-side with our fellow man, our neighbor, our brother, our sister. Prejudice, greed, pride, deception, corruption, and false motives have taken us to a point where the only way He could possibly get our attention was through a pandemic, economic strife, and an upheaval of humanity.

I hope we get that. And I hope we do more than raise our eyebrows and ask, "wow, what if that's true?" We need to act. We need to fix things. God gave us all gifts and talents. Don't waste them. Let's use them, even in some small way, to bring humanity back and love the little children *and* big children of the world—no matter what color.

*I wrote this the week George Floyd was murdered. I was hurting. I was mad. Mad at what had happened in Minneapolis. And mad at every other place these senseless, needless, unjustified killings of Black men and women were happening. Ferguson. The Bronx. Louisville. Brunswick.*

*Baltimore. Staten Island. Many others. Too many others. And mad at myself. Mad that I would simply shake my head or perhaps yell at the TV, and then just let life go on its way. But this one was different. It was a jolt. It was a call to action. I pledged to My Creator that day that complacency would no longer be my response. I made advocacy part of my personal and corporate mantra. I had a long way to go. I still do. But I'm trying.*

# Last Supper

**In March of 2020, my wife and I left our friendly confines** and drove two hours north to one of our favorite getaway towns. We had a bit of family business to address, but basically, we looked forward to downtown walks and a great dinner at one of our favorite scenic restaurants.

That was to be our final dinner out for the next year.

Our state shut down that weekend, and for the next fifty-two weeks, we were exposed to an existence only imagined by the likes of George Orwell or William Golding.[18]

I saw a lot of "a year ago", "before the pandemic", and "do you remember when" stories pop up over many months in all forms of media, no matter a person's leanings. For some, a rehash of that year can be as debilitating as the months themselves. They lost loved ones, jobs, businesses, savings, elections, stability. The term "essential workers" entered our lexicon on a daily basis as we watched health-care workers, first responders, and educators attempt to keep the country alive physically and emotionally.

We all wondered when and how it would end. Surely when the weather warms, the virus will dissipate much like the flu, because after all, the virus really is nothing more than a bit tougher version of the flu. Or so was the thinking, or hope, of many. (*Eighty-eight percent of those polled in March 2020 thought deaths would not exceed 10,000*).[19]

Warmer weather came. The virus continued. Events and arenas shut down. Sports leagues stopped or severely altered operation under stringent protocols. A Black man was murdered by a policeman in full video view before the first baseball was pitched. Then another. And another. People began to march against racial and social injustice.

And not just Black people. Anyone who cared. Most wore masks. Some didn't. Some fought back.

The presidential election became the most divisive of any in the last hundred-plus years, some say since the Civil War era itself. At a time when love thy neighbor was becoming more urgent than ever, many neighbors weren't talking to each other as they polarized on opposite sides of the spectrum. For some, Jim Crow was back. To others, Jim Crow had nothing to do with lost jobs, financial insecurity, and educational flip-flopping.

Deaths soared. Tempers flared. An insurrection occurred.

The roller coaster ride was not fun. It was way too long and had more ups, downs, and stomach-churning moments than we could, well, stomach.

We all looked to hit the pause button. We had to. Either because regulations said to or simply for our emotional mental health. It was time to collect ourselves, if that was even possible.

Ironically, a year to the day after our weekend to that town to the north, I received my second vaccine. I recalled that final dinner vividly.

As I took communion that week, I was struck by the similarities between the Last Supper and my last dinner. The disciples could not imagine what was coming. It was chaos. For a while. And then things became more clear. The best was yet to come albeit not without some very difficult work, faith and dedication.

I can't help but think there was a lot to learn from that year. I just hope I was paying enough attention to understand the need to roll up my sleeves and prepare to do the work.

We can do this.

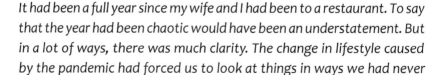

*It had been a full year since my wife and I had been to a restaurant. To say that the year had been chaotic would have been an understatement. But in a lot of ways, there was much clarity. The change in lifestyle caused by the pandemic had forced us to look at things in ways we had never before conceived. In some ways, that was quite uplifting. In other ways,*

the scabs of society revealed huge sores as they came off unveiling irritations with which many had difficulty coping or accepting. The world had gone awry. As we sat down for dinner every night, many wondered what was going to happen next. What was to come? I couldn't help but think that must have been much the way the disciples felt as Christ gathered them one last time before the most momentous events in the world were about to happen – his arrest, crucifixion and resurrection. Nothing like that had ever happened before. Or would again. Were they ready? Did they understand that what they were going through was necessary to prepare them for what was to come -- His resurrection and their life-changing ministries? The shock must have been unfathomable. All had been turned on its head. What was to come? What was to happen next? As we all sat amidst the confusion of a year surrounded by abnormality after abnormality, many of us wondered the same thing. Those who understood that God had a plan and was in control, were at peace and handling things a lot better. Others bordered on a state of apoplexy.

# As We All Sit Ringside

**A year ago...my, my that seems like forever-ago...I sat in** a room with friends. A new year had launched. The holidays were behind us. We were all optimistic.

There was chatter about the recent holidays. New Year resolutions. Plans for family trips. Events to look forward to. Predictions for our favorite sports teams. It was all so clear to us. Afterall, our vision was 2020.

Someone suggested we all chose a theme that would be our watchword for the coming year. Gratitude. Community. Focus. Impact. A host of others. All glorious goals to wrap our arms around.

I chose trust. Little did I realize the challenge I had just declared. I figured it would be a great focus. Wrap my arms around trust because as I grow gracefully older day by day, I learn I really can't control what I think I can control or what I'd like to control.

For a "planner" that's a difficult admission. I can be obsessive.

I habitually plan what time of day I can sit down to make tomorrow's plan—or next week's—or the week after. As my day begins early, I'm thinking with my still weary brain, what steps I make in the kitchen that will save me a few seconds here, a few minutes there so I can slide into my workday at the proper time.

I'm still an inveterate reader of the morning paper. I know. Give me a break here. It is delivered to the house Thursday through Sunday. The other days of the week, I hop in the car to buy one at the local convenience store. My goal is to get all the other stuff—breakfast, feed the cats, morning devotional—done so I can be out the door somewhere between 4:51 and 4:53. If it's past 4:55, I begin to fidget.

Yes, obsessive about planning.

So, it will come as no surprise if I admit to a whole lot of introspection when it comes to trust and how I make decisions through the course of the day and week.

To trust, one must understand that God has a plan and that God's timing is perfect. Not my plan. His plan. Not my timing. His timing.

Some people don't believe in God. That's sad. Some people believe in a Supreme Being, but don't have the pleasure and comfort of carrying Him in their heart, allowing Him to change the heart, direct, comfort and heal. I get that. Letting go of control may be the most difficult thing any one does.

Letting go and trusting leads to how we make decisions. Without trust, we decide what's best for us and plan that course. Other times, we simply react or must decide with relatively little notice when an incident or situation rears its head.

If we're lucky, we get most of those right. If we're not, woe to the decision-maker. Discontent. Suffering. Discomfort.

But after all the trials, travails and challenges of the Covid era, and we all know what they have been, I'm beginning to think there may be a better way to move forward. Oh, sure. Trust is still vital.

We need unification of spirit and healing, both literal and figurative. If we are to change divisiveness, greed, inequality, inequity, selfishness, self-righteousness, and a whole litany of society's ills, we need to make a conscious decision to do just that.

I sometimes live in my own little world. I try to be nice and kind and smile a lot.

I handle what's on my plate. I handle what comes to me. I help others if a situation rears its head where I can do that. But I don't go looking for it.

Moving forward, I want to be serious about making a difference, about making change, about helping people who need help, about understanding society's ills better, and challenging some of them. I can't simply wait until they come to me or until I'm impacted by them.

I need to make a clear-cut decision to step out of my comfort zone. I need to fight more for change. I need to answer the bell that is going off in my head that says more can be done. I need to be intentional.

Yes, that is going to be my word this year. Intentional.

*It became very apparent to me during the pandemic that I could either sit around and wait for things to get better or take a look at what I could perhaps help fix. But to do that, I couldn't just identify certain things. I had to be willing to act. I had to be* **intentional**. *If I wanted my voice to be heard for social and racial injustice, I needed to do more than simply write "thoughts for daily living." I needed to understand better what my Black brothers and sisters had gone through and how they were still being impacted. I could read, but that still wasn't enough. I had to get to know them better—more of them. That meant putting myself in a situation where I was around more Black people and was not reluctant to be among the minority. That's more than simply saying that I have a Black neighbor, and I think he's a great guy. That's more than saying I always make it a point to go up to the Black family visiting church to introduce myself and welcome them. It's more than having a gathering at the house and being sure I invite one Black couple. It's not being afraid, and sometimes forcing myself to be the only white person in the room. So, I began attending a predominantly Black church. I attended tours of our city's predominantly Black neighborhoods under gentrification. I insisted on dining in those neighborhoods even though I was asked by a colleague after inquiring of a good place to eat whether I was okay with being the only White person in the restaurant. Intentional. I had to push myself to do something out of the norm. The only way we begin to understand racial and social injustice is to put ourselves in the throes of those who experience it—each and every day. Then observe. And listen.*

# I Never Knew

**Have you ever been surprised or startled by what** someone tells you?

Perhaps, it's a friend with a confession. *Do I really want to know that?*

Maybe it's a spouse telling you that outfit really isn't "you." *What do you mean green is not my color?*

Perhaps it's from the mouth of babes. I had a friend confess that once when he spoke to a third-grade class and asked for questions, the first one was, "Why are you so fat?"

Maybe it's a colleague asking you where you bought the perfume or cologne you're wearing. Then suggesting you take it back. *Hmmm. What's he or she really trying to tell me?* You can laugh or be offended. The call is yours.

What if you tell someone that you're excited to be going on a vacation because you hadn't taken one in six years, and there is a long pause. You're expecting her shock at the six long years and hoping for an acknowledgement of shared enthusiasm. Instead, you get, "I've never been on a vacation."

At first, you may think she's joking. Then you realize that given her life circumstances, it's probably true. Her voids have been more than vacations. And now, it's you with the long pause.

It's easy to get so caught up in our own world, that we think everyone acts like us, lives like us, believes like us, thinks like us and has the opportunity to experience the same things we do. But unfortunately, we live in a society of extremes. Economic extremes. Educational extremes. Emotional extremes. Opportunity extremes.

In an effort to show empathy, you say something like, "Well, I know that will soon change," or "I know you will get the chance real soon," or "Well, if you could, where would you go?"

And the next response is not what you expect either.

Not the beach. Not the mountains. Not the lake. Not Las Vegas. Not Europe. Not the Islands. Not Disney World.

"I think I'd like go visit my dad since I haven't seen him in twenty years."

You are getting more and more uncomfortable. *Now what do I say?* You blurt out, "Where does your dad live?"

She responds, "I'm not sure. When he got out of prison two years ago, he never let me know where he was going."

Finally, simply overcome with an inability to relate, you blurt out, "Oh my, dear. I'm so sorry. I'll pray for you."

Her response, "I never knew you were a Christian."

Ouch.

---

*These are the moments I feel I'm just not measuring up. I think I'm doing and saying all the right things—showing compassion, interest, care, grace and all those other wonderful attributes. I'm reminded every day that non-Christians do many wonderful things as well. I certainly hope to get to the point with a colleague or acquaintance where they tell me how much they appreciate my attention and helpful hand, and I'm able to share the reason for that—a change of heart that only Christ can provide. But it's kinda like the quarterback who leads by example. He's not showy. Makes all the right calls. Doesn't take credit for the wins. Willing to take the blame for the miscues. But he never says what makes him tick. And if those around him don't know, they can be easily swayed by a firebrand leader who inspires through false bravado, but can't ever quite get it done. To get it done, one ultimately has to proclaim, what makes one tick. And deliver.*

# The Road and the Thermos

**I have always liked Robert Frost. *The Road Not Taken*.**[20]
This standard high school poem reading ends, "I took the one less traveled by and that has made all the difference."

That has always spoken to me even though, admittedly, there have been times in my life where the road less traveled has not proved the best or the correct path.

We learn.

What seems logical, often isn't. What seems brave and daring is often reckless. Inspiration often fades quickly.

We come to a fork, two paths, and wonder, "Which is the correct one?"

What do we do? How do we handle it? What helps us make that decision?

The faith community often has the same dilemma.

"Gosh, that's odd," say some. "Doesn't God direct your path constantly if you live in faith? Doesn't that conviction and moral compass help you choose the right path?"

Well. Yes. Sort of.

For many, the walk of faith is one of boldness and courage.

"Let's see what type of God-statement we can make. Let's not be afraid to take the road less traveled. God will be with us. God will direct us."

We think we hear His direction so clearly. We proceed. Then the path gets narrower. Fallen trees and thistles overcome it. We slip and fall as the road heads down a steep hill. It starts to get dark. We think we hear wild animals nearby. Perhaps it's time to abort and rethink our course.

So, what are we hearing? Why has the path become so cumbersome? Did we choose incorrectly? We were so sure when we started down the road that this path was God's direction. Clarity becomes more difficult to ascertain.

Is He trying to tell me that I have chosen the wrong road and that I really wasn't listening when I came to that fork? Was I thinking I wanted this route because by conquering it, there would be reward for me at the end—reward that was perhaps more my reward than His reward?

Or, have the obstacles come simply because He wants to see how much trust I will have that He will lead me from my questionable and difficult state, providing answers if I am faithful and stay the course?

I sometimes wish choosing a path was like reading the thermostat so I know if the path is hot or cold, easy or hard, God's will or not. The thermos can figure out which is which. Why is it so difficult for me?

I'm told that eventually you know, and God uses both circumstances for growth. But I want to know. Now. Which I guess is one of the flaws of the road less traveled. You want to know right from the outset how it's all going to come out. And that's not for you to know.

---

*As an English major, I always loved literature that spoke words with hidden meanings and metaphorical insights. But decisions and consequences can be tough. Sometimes we proceed tepidly. With caution. Sometimes, we move boldly. Sometimes, we guess right. Other times, we guess wrong. For those of us of faith, we really shouldn't be simply guessing. We take key situations, decisions, and opportunities to God and allow him to speak to us. But what if He doesn't speak. What if we don't hear anything. Does that mean that He isn't there? That He doesn't care?*

*The Bible says not to lean on our own understanding, so perhaps we tread lightly. Does the decision or direction need to be made right now? Do we read God's tea leaves as saying "wait" or "not yet?" Does the decision seem so very clear to us that we are certain that it's God* directing our path, only to fail? Did we fail because it was actually "us" who wanted that path? We wanted it so badly and convinced ourselves it would be so good for us that surely God must be involved somehow? Or was the path such a rough one that we learned things we needed to learn and apply later in life?

I once was convinced that God wanted me to start a company. I worked diligently for nearly two years to prepare for that launch. I did countless hours of research and calculations. I slept barely four hours a night burning the midnight oil. I was convinced He wanted me to have a successful business. Afterall, it would be a business founded and led by Christian principles. I would dutifully tithe, thanking him for all my success. I would become both a beacon of the community and the church. Everyone would marvel about my corporate, financial and spiritual acumen. But it didn't happen that way. The business blew up. I was nearly a million dollars in debt. My marriage crashed. What happened? I had chosen the difficult path convinced that God would bless me. But it was "my" path and not "his" path. The thistles had overcome my path. The wild animals had eaten me. The path back was not an easy one. But at least I learned to listen. And here I am. The soul whole again.

# Don't Give Me That Crap

**The good. The bad. The ugly.**

That's what a lot of people believe constitutes life - society's ills. Those in community service address them every day - those brave enough to get out of their comfort zones and impact society. In their own little way.

Politics. Left. Right. Red. Blue. Government rules and regulations. Efforts to legislate morality.

It all makes one's head spin. Why can't we all just get along?

Then there are moments and examples of kindness, heroism, altruism, and downright uplifting stories of humanity - people helping each other. Strangers stepping to the plate. Embraces between new-found allies and comfort givers.

I recently told a colleague I really cherished those "God moments." He pushed back. We were politically aligned, but he resisted my faith overture.

"Don't give me that religious crap. I see more good things being done by non-Christians than I do Christians," he uttered frankly. "I don't think faith or Christianity have anything to do with why people do good things. As a matter of fact, I've seen a lot more kind and gracious acts from my Muslim, Hindu, Jewish and agnostic friends than I've seen from my so-called Christian acquaintances."

He then launched into a long array of grievances.

"I get tired of hearing so-called Christians take positions against helpless immigrants because they believe their own 'God-given' culture will be overrun or that it will impact them economically. Or reticent to admit that Black lives matter, too, holding instead to a perception that a race taken advantage of for more than 400 years is being too aggressive about picking society's scabs. Or trying their damndest to rationalize away legitimate environmental and health-related crises as hoaxes. Or not even wanting to recognize economic, educational and healthcare inequities. Or talk about the wealth gap. Or even step out of their comfortable little lives to help someone across the street or load their groceries. All that and more tell me they are anything but interested in the 'least of these' and fixing the ills of society."

Whew! That was a lot. Yes, he was shooting pretty much from his political hip. But it was difficult to argue with him.

As he saw Christians, particularly in the political arena, taking positions that he firmly believed were non-Christian stances, I began to understand his reticence to hear the Gospel.

He had read the Sermon on the Mount.[21] He wondered why those proclaiming to be Christians didn't adhere more to the direct teaching of the One they professed to follow.

I sensed an opportunity. But probably not now. He was too jaded. I was probably going to have to show him by actions instead of words for a while.

Maybe I need to help someone with their groceries.

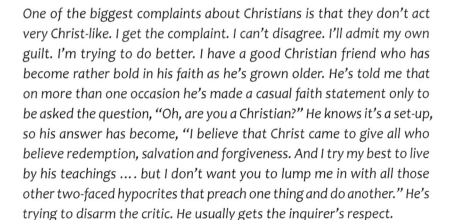

*One of the biggest complaints about Christians is that they don't act very Christ-like. I get the complaint. I can't disagree. I'll admit my own guilt. I'm trying to do better. I have a good Christian friend who has become rather bold in his faith as he's grown older. He's told me that on more than one occasion he's made a casual faith statement only to be asked the question, "Oh, are you a Christian?" He knows it's a set-up, so his answer has become, "I believe that Christ came to give all who believe redemption, salvation and forgiveness. And I try my best to live by his teachings .... but I don't want you to lump me in with all those other two-faced hypocrites that preach one thing and do another." He's trying to disarm the critic. He usually gets the inquirer's respect.*

*As we look at the ills of society as laid out by the accuser in the text, it's interesting how we begin to make political rather than spiritual evaluations on each. We shouldn't. But we do. Perhaps my friend's retort, that many Christians might criticize as a copout, is a lot more on point than many think. If we would just go see what the Scriptures say about those ills then try to fix them with a genuine love in our heart, we might begin to quit playing sides. And politics. And begin acting more Christ-like.*

# Around the Room

**It always began the same way. The seven men exchanging** greetings and perfunctory evaluations of the prior week at the leader's cue.

"Does anyone have anything he wants to share this week? Needs? Blessings? Prayer requests? Concerns?"

Bill began as James bowed his head.

"Tough week. My supervisor has been busting my chops all week. He's new and I think he sees me as a threat. I'm really not, even though I'm a lot more experienced than he is. So, I guess I need your prayers on how to relate to him. How to communicate that to him. I really need to keep my job."

Darren went next.

"My kids have some really tough tests coming up this week. They get all up in knots when it's test time. They just put so much pressure on themselves. All their friends are getting into the best colleges, and they have this fear that if they get anything less than an A, their life will end. My kids mean everything to me. I just want them to do well and be successful."

Roger was up.

"My wife and I are having a hard time deciding where to go on our vacation this summer. I want to go to Maine because we've never been there. She wants to go to Napa. We're having a hard time reaching an agreement on this. I don't like disagreements. My wife and I should be on the same page. I guess I just need to drop the hint that she needs to follow my lead on this. So, pray for her...us."

David came next.

"I really need a new car. The old Benz is costing too much to maintain. Our budget is taking a real hit with all those repairs. As a matter of fact, we're a bit out over our skis with several things right now. So, pray we can get a better grip on our finances."

James, his head still bowed.

"I'm going to pass. Wrestling with a lot. But I just want to pass tonight."

Rick took it and ran.

"I have a tough decision to make. My wife and I have been invited to my niece's wedding this weekend, and I don't want to go. She's marrying a Black man, and I'm not sure where she stands in her walk with God. She has a lot of tattoos and seems to me to have a lot of issues. I'm not comfortable with all that. So, pray I come up with the right words to explain why we can't be there."

The leader wrapped up all the prayer requests neatly with a special emphasis on James' unspoken needs.

James continued to pray silently.

"Not a single request for anyone other than ourselves. Lord, forgive us. There are so many needy in the world around us and so many needing what you can provide. Yet, all too often, all we think about are our needs and wants. Forgive us for our selfishness and blinders."

*I wish I could say that I just made this up. But I didn't. This was the experience I had when I joined a men's worship group a few years ago. My angst every week was seeing so many people in need around the community, and all we seemed to worry about was our own little world. We never talked about getting out into the community let alone actually doing it. Much of the perspective was on the doctrine of the denomination, and I wasn't exactly buying all that either. I began to wonder why Christians spend so much time trying to dissect and interpret the scriptures than genuinely trying to live them. And I wondered why "outreach" only came within the boundaries of the church programs rather than encouraging "the flock" to find a cause or need in the community*

about which one was passionate and become involved. Seems that would be a great way to demonstrate our faith. With works. Let those in need wonder why we do what we do. And ask us. So, we can share. Let them see that we are Christians by our love. Not our doctrine.

# Grace

**The young man was shabbily dressed. He wandered** around town, a smile on his face. A giddy-up in his step. Except when he was tired.

Many wondered where he had come from. Where did he live? What did he do? Where did he hang out? Who were his friends?

He didn't seem to be wanton for anything. Yet, many wondered why he didn't have a car, dress better, or at least eat at decent restaurants.

Some said he was a pastor who had come to town. But when pressed, they really couldn't name the church with which he was affiliated.

But people seemed to like him. He always seemed to have a few people hanging with him. Every so often, a group would gather around him at the local park. Everyone would just sit and listen to the young man tell story after story.

"Man, you ought to write a book," one declared. "That's some pretty heavy stuff you're talking about. I think more people need to hear that."

The young man encouraged them to reach into the community. "Make sure you leave this world a better place than when you entered," he'd say.

One day, he came upon a woman sitting under a tree. She was forlorn. Weak. Appeared as if she may have been there the entire night. Her skin was ashen.

He approached slowly and gently bent over.

"Are you okay?" he asked. He already knew the answer.

She feigned a smile and muttered that she would be okay. He knew otherwise. He told her to rest comfortably for a few minutes. He would get them both something to drink. Then, they could talk.

She thanked him.

While away, he called his friend Luke who was a doctor. He asked if Luke would meet him at the tree. The young man arrived first. Luke shortly thereafter.

She was reticent to go with the men. But she was weak. She really could not resist. They helped her to Luke's car. Luke took her to his office.

"I can't repay you," she told him. "And I'm pregnant. If you can't help me, at least save my baby." Luke was quiet. She wasn't sure he had heard her. The young man stood nearby.

"Her kidneys are failing," said Luke. "I'm going to put her on dialysis, but she needs a transplant. And soon."

"How does that work?" asked the young man. "Can she have a transplant if she's expecting?"

"Yes. It's tricky. But, first, we need to find a match."

"Test me," replied the young man.

Luke began the testing procedure. He warned him that matches were rare. Yet for some reason, they matched.

A few days later, one of the young man's kidneys was moved from his body to the woman's. The doctors said the surgery went well.

The young man went back to wandering the town and the parks, but he returned a week later to see the woman.

"I can't believe what you did for me," she uttered. "You didn't even know me. You gave me life. I can't repay you."

He smiled. What she and the doctors didn't know was that his other kidney was defective. He would be dead within months. He really had given his life for her.

As her daughter grew, she would often ask her mother about the mysterious young man.

"I don't know that much about him, Grace. All I know is that he gave his life for you and me."

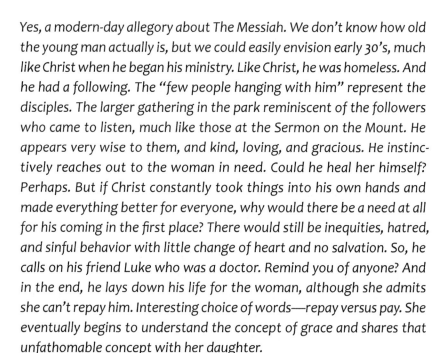

*Yes, a modern-day allegory about The Messiah. We don't know how old the young man actually is, but we could easily envision early 30's, much like Christ when he began his ministry. Like Christ, he was homeless. And he had a following. The "few people hanging with him" represent the disciples. The larger gathering in the park reminiscent of the followers who came to listen, much like those at the Sermon on the Mount. He appears very wise to them, and kind, loving, and gracious. He instinctively reaches out to the woman in need. Could he heal her himself? Perhaps. But if Christ constantly took things into his own hands and made everything better for everyone, why would there be a need at all for his coming in the first place? There would still be inequities, hatred, and sinful behavior with little change of heart and no salvation. So, he calls on his friend Luke who was a doctor. Remind you of anyone? And in the end, he lays down his life for the woman, although she admits she can't repay him. Interesting choice of words—repay versus pay. She eventually begins to understand the concept of grace and shares that unfathomable concept with her daughter.*

*Grace, the gift of healing and eternal salvation. It is totally undeserved. One can't perform works to obtain it. It can't be repaid. Through his incomprehensible love, God washes away all wrongdoing for those whom understand that his son, Jesus, died and put the sins of all mankind on himself. With that understanding and acceptance, lifestyle and hearts are changed and salvation cemented.*

# SOCIAL & SPIRITUAL AWARENESS

# Woman in the Park

**The woman was sitting quietly on the park bench. She** overlooked a quiet pond. The wind was blowing quietly. Everything about that moment was quiet. Except her soul.

She was in great distress. None of her dots were connecting. Her lover had walked away. Her dad had died. Mom was very ill. She had no siblings with whom to bond. She had lost her job of ten years. Money would soon trickle to nothing. She was behind on her rent payments.

She bowed her head to talk to God - but she really wasn't sure anymore that there even was such a person, thing, force, or whatever God was supposed to be.

As time passed, all around she saw children playing. Lovers holding hands. Grandmothers pushing kids in strollers. She had none of that. How long had she been sitting there? She had lost all track of time.

A woman walked by and smiled. The woman on the bench lifted her head and feigned a return expression. The other woman stopped. And slowly returned.

"Hey. Are you all right?" she asked, sensing pain in the woman's eyes. The woman on the bench said nothing at first. She slowly looked up, a small tear trickling down one cheek.

"No. No, I'm not."

The other woman sat down. She put a hand on the distressed woman's leg. It felt good to be touched, thought the quiet woman.

"Do you want to talk about it?"

"No. I can't," came the response.

The other woman said that was okay. She remained by her side. She continued to touch her. She, too, looked out onto the park...the quiet pond...listening to the wind. Minutes passed.

"You know," said the second woman. "I used to come to this park years ago. I haven't been here in a long, long time. But I used to come here a lot. To listen."

"What did you listen to?" asked the first.

"I wasn't sure at first. I just knew that if I listened long enough, God would speak to me."

"How did you know it was God?" asked the first.

"Oh. You know. You know because a great sense of calm and peace comes over you. And I often even walked away with an action plan or two. And they often worked."

"I don't know. I don't know if that will work for me."

"It may not at first," said the woman still communicating through touch as well as words. "But if you are willing to accept that it might, you are one step closer.

"There is chaos everywhere," she continued. "I've lived that chaos. Every single moment. I tried to escape that chaos by taking my own life. And then someone said, 'meet me at the park'."

"Who was that person?" asked the first woman.

"Good question. It wasn't a person at all. It was simply a voice directing my path. So, I came here. Sat. Listened. You can do this. But you don't have to do it alone. I think that was the key message I heard as I, too, looked onto that pond."

For the first time, the shaken woman turned to look into the other woman's eyes. She saw someone who cared. She saw hope. She embraced the woman and actually smiled.

She continued to come to that park bench every week. But now she came with a purpose. To listen.

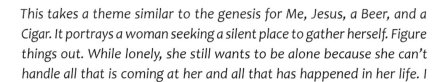

*This takes a theme similar to the genesis for Me, Jesus, a Beer, and a Cigar. It portrays a woman seeking a silent place to gather herself. Figure things out. While lonely, she still wants to be alone because she can't handle all that is coming at her and all that has happened in her life. I*

*attempt to portray quiet because, for me, that is when I most often get ideas and hear God speak.*

*There are some subtleties with the second woman I don't want you to miss. First, she comes without being announced—much like God. She sees a need to show compassion and recognizes a hurting soul. She admits she has not been to that park in a long, long time, a place where many years ago she, too, came to find answers. What possessed her to be there that day? And she intuitively knows that physically touching the other woman will create a powerful connection. I often believe that among our five senses, touch can be the game changer. So, the woman touches her almost from the start and doesn't stop—analogous to how Christ touches us and doesn't stop even if we are unwilling to listen.*

*At one point, the listening woman realizes that she, too, needs to be quiet as both women gather themselves and let their thoughts and emotions percolate. In an era when many of us believe that doing more and more, constantly being active and in motion, is the way to keep ahead of all that is coming at us, this entry shows the necessity of seeking the quiet.*

# The Project

**DeRon Williams was a bastard. Literally.**

His mom was raped when she was a teenager. She already had two small children. She worked three jobs. When she could. Her Aunt Juju lived with her. Juju watched the kids. Most of the time. But Juju liked to have fun sometimes. Afterall, she was only thirty-five.

They lived in the projects. The projects. You know – those areas cities have set aside as subsidized housing where they can keep all the depraved in one spot. It's easier for the police that way.

The community's average income was poverty level. Subsidized food was a necessity. Even when one tried to work three jobs. DeRon and his mom were caught in that cycle.

By the time DeRon was six, he had three more brothers and sisters. Juju and his mom sent him to school each day to get a decent meal and to get away from sinister "elements" that roamed the neighborhood.

DeRon never really liked school. His attention span was short. His mind always seemed distracted by something. He tried to make friends, but to do that, you had to prove you were worthy. Bravado reigned the day.

By the time he was in middle school, he was being recruited. He wasn't an athlete. Although he thought he was tough. He showed he was tough by talking back to Juju and his mom. They asked if he had homework. No. Well, okay then.

Out the door he'd go. To the recruiters. All the recruiters had money and, even better yet – girls. And man, they were hot! He wasn't sure where they got their clothes, but they were certainly stylin' like real divas.

A few thought he was cute. Put their hands on him. Kissed his neck. He liked that. Then they would pull away. Teasing him. He didn't like that.

Soon he succumbed to the recruiters. Soon he was earning good money, too. Mom and Juju wondered where it was coming from. But not really. He was buying them things. He even bought his mom a new car. Well, a new used car. It beat taking the metro.

He quit going to school. He began to hang out with Daphne. She had a little boy, so DeRon knew she knew how to "do it." He wanted to do it. Things heated up one night. Really hot. Then Daphne pushed him away. DeRon got really mad. His recruiters laughed. Told him to go take it out on some white chick.

He did.

DeRon just raped your daughter. Who do you blame?

She's pregnant. What do you do?

*There's a lot to unpack here. First there is the underlying theme of systemic racism—how America pushed Blacks into areas of a city where it could control them, but not provide any significant assistance. While White city officials called it subsidized housing, the areas became known as "the projects." Everyone who didn't live there knew to keep away. They were poverty stricken and crime infested. White logic said that poverty led to crime.*

*These people really had no chance. No choice. The system worked 100 percent against them. Some claim that there are plenty of instances where people have fought their way out of the projects to become productive citizens. And there have been. But how many? And against what odds? And what was the trigger that led to that better life?*

*DeRon's mother clearly was no influence. Sure, she tried to work to keep food on the table. But she, herself was promiscuous, taken advantage of, and experienced the violence within her community. Men see promiscuity as a right to push things all the way, whether the woman* wants to or not. Afterall, her history and lifestyle proved she wanted it—or so the thinking goes.

DeRon really had no chance growing up. No one showed him right from wrong. No one talked to him about God. No one showed him love. No one ever encouraged or believed in him.

The result is not only devastating, but criminal. So, the system perpetuates itself. But that's not all that's here. A middle-class White girl has been raped and impregnated. What do we do with that? Blame DeRon? Send him to prison? Blame the system? Then how are you going to fix it? And how long will that take? Far easier to send DeRon away, like thousands and thousands of others, and let someone else worry about fixing the system.

You have a daughter to worry about. She's been brutally raped. Pregnant. Psychologically maimed. She abhors the fertilized seed within her. It reminds her every minute of every day of the horror of that moment. What do you do? Satan's seed has been planted within. What do you, as a born-again Christian, do? What will state laws allow you to do?

And that's what makes abortion so complicated. It's not as cut and dry as many try to make it. I have much angst with those so eager to condemn abortion but show no willingness to correct many of the systemic circumstances that perpetuate the evils of society that lead to many other unnecessary deaths.

Finally, the title itself. The Project. While tendency is to think it refers to the housing area where DeRon and family lived, it actually insinuates that there is much work to be done. When one thinks of a project, one thinks of something that will take a while to develop but has a clear plan in place to get there. The between-the-lines irony questions whether the project of making life better for those in the projects has any plan at all since the cycle continues to perpetuate itself. Yes, it is a project, indeed.

# Just a Note Off

**It was a fourth-floor walk-up on the Lower East Side.**
Every Saturday, I descended to the street and looked both ways. It was still early. Calm. Relatively. Fewer taxi horn blasts. Even fewer sirens.

And there was Zamir. Playing his harmonica aided by a sound system that made his sound almost philharmonic. He was good.

A shoebox sat next to him on the sidewalk. A few coins and dollars were already starting to appear. Neighbors passed by with coffee and bagels in hand.

His sign said that he couldn't find a job. He was hungry. Had a family to support. It didn't say he was homeless. He may have been too embarrassed to share that. His clothes were fairly kept. Hair a bit tousled.

Normally, I would just smile and wave at Zamir. Perhaps throw some loose change or a buck in his shoebox.

The weather was cool this fall morning. I knew that winter was not very far away. I wondered what Zamir did when it became icy cold. Where he would go. I wondered about his family. I wondered why it was tough for him to get a job. I wondered what other skills Zamir had other than playing that harmonica.

I walked to the end of the block. Grabbed a hot venti. Black. No sugar or cream. I found the jolt perfect for that time of day.

Today, however, I decided I would do something I normally didn't do. I stopped to talk to Zamir. He wasn't very conversive at first. He simply wanted to continue to play that harmonica as his shoe box began to fill with coins and paper. He finally smiled and stopped as my hands formed a "T" to signal timeout.

He took a breather and turned off the sound system. We tried to converse. I asked him where he was from. About his family. What he did in real life. I told him I wanted to help. I told him I loved his music.

Zamir said he was from Albania. I asked if his dialect was Tosk or Gheg. He said Tosk, seemingly impressed that I even knew to ask the question. He was embarrassed that his English was so poor. He said he's only been in New York a short time. He had no family ties. Finding Tosk speakers had been difficult so far.

I asked how I could reach him. If he had a cell phone. He did not. All he seemed to have was his harmonica and that shoe box. He pretended to not understand when I asked him where he lived. Perhaps, he was embarrassed. I could tell the conversation was winding down.

I smiled. Put my hands together to indicate I would pray for him. Then put a ten-spot in the shoebox. He said thank you in his broken English then began harmonic-ing again. He sure could play.

As I wandered back to my walk-up, I felt I had to do more than just pray for Zamir. That's actually rather easy. But Zamir and his family needed more than prayers. They needed intervention, help.

I opened my laptop and jumped on the neighborhood social site. I asked if anyone knew anything about Zamir. His circumstances. Then, for resources to help him. A job. Someone who spoke Albanian Tosk.

The replies were mixed, but overwhelmingly warning that Zamir was a fake. His harmonica playing was a scam, they said. The sound system wasn't there to complement his playing but to hide his lack of skill and talent. Instead of trying to help, it was suggested I call the police. Surely there must be some loitering laws or something.

I was a bit taken aback. Had I been deceived? Did these neighbors know more about Zamir than I did? I probed. Some said they had challenged him. He feigned poor English. One pulled the plug on his sound system. Zamir kept playing. He wasn't bad, although far less audible.

A few weeks later, I did my typical Saturday plod down four flights on my way to the coffee shop. There was no Zamir. Nor the next week. Or the next week. I hoped a job had taken him away from his shoebox.

I asked someone at the coffee shop. She said the neighbors ran him off, filing a panhandling grievance.

I was sad. I really didn't care if Zamir was a fake or not. That wasn't the point. The point was that he seemed to need help. If he was indeed scamming the system, shame on him. Although, he didn't have that vibe to me.

Had I turned my back on someone in need? Could I have done more? Could I have perhaps come to his defense? I knew the answer. Shame on me. And on his accusers for casting judgment and not wanting to learn more about Zamir.

He sure could play.

If you've done it to one of the least of these, my brethren ...

*I don't exactly remember when I became convicted about reaching out to help those on the streets. Since that happened, I've tried to become more intentional about it. Admittedly, I don't stop at every sign holder or stop what I'm doing to comb every in-city neighborhood where the pickings are easy, but I do wonder about the "why" behind a person's circumstances.*

*When I stop, I usually ask questions to learn a bit about that person's life and circumstances. Some share. Some don't. I always end with asking them if they know why I'm providing a bit of financial help. If I get a blank stare, I tell them it is because that's what Christ would do for me—and then encourage them to find a place where they can learn more about Jesus. I've received a few twinkles in return.*

*In this story, we have an immigrant who has made it to the big city with his family. He knows hardly anyone. His language is creating barriers. But he has a talent, so he takes it to the street because at this time it's all he knows to do to collect a little money for food, shelter, clothing. And shelter isn't a given.*

But he's seen as an outsider by many who wander by. A panhandler. But they have taken no time to get to know him. Or if they have, they come with preconceived, hostile perceptions. Anger. Hardened hearts. Perhaps a touch of racial bias.

To me, I appreciate his skill and talent. Some try to twist his circumstance and say he's taking advantage of a system. What system is that? One that reaches out and helps people in need? As Zamir's shoe box fills up, it is apparent that many people want to help him out – and get joy from his harmonica playing.

Yet there are others who believe Zamir is up to something nefarious. They feel he is stealing.

Okay. Let's flip the script a bit and say that Zamir's sound system allows him to seem more talented than he really is. Yes, he is being deceptive. But is that any reason to overlook his situation? His need? Perhaps you've caught a young lad stealing a loaf of bread from the kitchen. Is the answer to punish him. Or to help him survive?

Too often we believe that teaching a person the hard lessons of life is the best thing we can do for them. Teach them right from wrong. But somehow, somewhere, I believe Jesus is flipping that script.

Seems mercy, love, grace should all come before retribution—no matter what the circumstances.

# Race Competition

**Sometimes we don't know, what we don't know.**

I hate to admit it. I fall into that category sometimes. I try to read a lot. Watch educational news and programming. (Give me *60 Minutes* every day!) Listen. Reflect. Contemplate. Pray. But sometimes I still don't quite get it.

Then there are times when what I thought I knew and believed is off a bit. More learning.

> race (verb): to compete against participants of various abilities

> race (noun): a competition among participants of various ethnicities

Okay, Merriam Webster doesn't actually give similar definitions for both the verb and noun version of race. But think about it.

Is there not a competition among people who don't look like each other to prove themselves? To compete?

What color shoe do you put on to run that race? The White one? Black one? Brown one? Red one? Yellow one? Multi-colored one?

How do you know if that race will be competitive? Or fair?

If we are being honest, and open to learning, we know the answer. The race is always influenced by conditions. Especially if it is the noun. Too often systemic.

In my effort to grasp more about races, I've attempted to learn, and really comprehend circumstances that were unfamiliar to me, often hidden from my eyes and understanding.

Those efforts have led to new and eye-opening friendships.

I recently met a Black brother for breakfast. He was trying to learn too. I was humbled by his desire to try to figure things out because from my vantage point, it was me who needed a lesson in perspective. I soon got one.

He grew up in Ferguson, MO. One of his family members mentored Michael Brown[22] before that fateful night. My new friend shared a tale that was common to him. All I could do was listen. I kept repeating the same word.

"Really?"

"Really?"

When he and his friends would go out at night in Ferguson, they would see the blue lights behind them at least once a month. The police questioned them. They demanded to know the boys' names. Asked for ID. Asked what they were doing. If they had drugs. If they'd been drinking. Asked if they had guns. Made sure all the "paperwork" was in order. Then, after not finding anything incriminating enough to continue the hassle, claim that they'd received a report of a car that looked just like the one the boys were driving as being stolen or involved in a robbery or some other illicit activity.

One night, the boys were in an old 1979 orange Firebird. The cops found nothing. Gave the same excuse for pulling them over.

All the guys in the car looked at each and thought simultaneously, "Really? Another car that looks just like this orange Firebird?" There may have been six in all North America.

By then, my friend's mom had given her son "the talk." But this was the final straw. She stormed down to the police station to say enough was enough. She wanted answers to why her son and his friends were constantly being pulled over.

Someone broke ranks. Confided in her that the police were instructed to pull over any car after a certain hour with two or more Black men. If they couldn't find anything, use the "car that looked just like this one" excuse, then write it up to keep track. SOP. Standard Operating Procedure.

Black boys. Not White boys.

I was pulled over by the police once as a teenager. I had been doing something I should not have been doing. The policeman knew it. He put me in his car and took me home. I wonder if that would have happened if I'd been Black?

I hurt when I hear stories like this. Sure, I read or hear about them most every day. But when you know someone that it has happened to, well, you get a different take.

It probably wasn't easy for my new friend to share that story with me. But I'm glad he did. I know he has others. I can't wait to do breakfast again.

There is a lot more to learn.

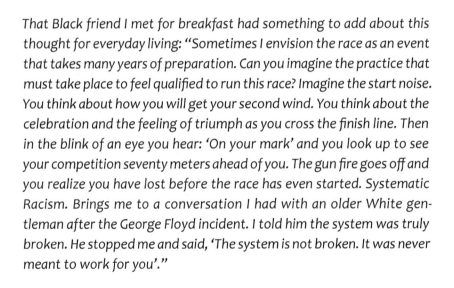

*That Black friend I met for breakfast had something to add about this thought for everyday living: "Sometimes I envision the race as an event that takes many years of preparation. Can you imagine the practice that must take place to feel qualified to run this race? Imagine the start noise. You think about how you will get your second wind. You think about the celebration and the feeling of triumph as you cross the finish line. Then in the blink of an eye you hear: 'On your mark' and you look up to see your competition seventy meters ahead of you. The gun fire goes off and you realize you have lost before the race has even started. Systematic Racism. Brings me to a conversation I had with an older White gentleman after the George Floyd incident. I told him the system was truly broken. He stopped me and said, 'The system is not broken. It was never meant to work for you'."*

# Storms and Pollution

**Yes. Metaphorical, indeed.**

I doubt I will get little pushback to say that 2020 was a year for the ages. One not soon forgotten. Although we all would like to. COVID-19. Economic free fall. Racial Unrest. Divisive election.

Seems like the only storms and pollution missing were the locust plague and the rivers turning to blood.

Not to over-complicate or over-stress the situation, but what about actual storms and pollution?

The year 2020 sent us the most severe weather patterns to date. Thirty named tropical storms and hurricanes. Twelve landfall hurricanes. Six "major" hurricanes. Five category-5 hurricanes (most ever in one season). Fifth consecutive year for a Cat-5. And billions of dollars of damage. Talk about being clobbered.

And yet there's more.

Global temperatures were the warmest on record due to the burning of fossil fuels. Seas rose 3.2 millimeters and Greenland's ice-shelf shed enough of its glaciers in just two months to result in a 2.2-millimeter rise (1 metric ton *per minute*) around its coastline.[23]

Up to ten million people died worldwide as a result of air pollution. Another nine million will die of starvation while one-third of the food intended for consumption—1.3 million tons—goes wasted. Enough to feed three billion people.[24]

Storms and pollution.

Every day we experience the scars of physical pollution. But perhaps even more catastrophic are the scars of emotional and character pollution. We often seek blame instead of solutions.

We shake our heads and bow our neck as we try to manage the crises that we see and read about every day in the news. It's tough some days.

I wonder how many of us have broken down and cried.

Perhaps it's unfair to heap bad news and cite statistics about climate and hunger, when we are doing the best we can to just get to the next year.

Many believe, and perhaps rightly so, that the four big calamities cited earlier will eventually sort themselves out. And they might.

But let's hope that the storms and pollution in our own lives don't keep us from understanding that there is much more to fix than those that are immediately touching us. Devastation is all around us, and there really is only one solution.

I've believed from the beginning that God had a plan and wanted to get our attention by throwing all the setbacks of 2020 at us. He wasn't happy. He wanted to see how we would respond. He wanted us to figure out what is really important. In many instances, we have not fared well and have not figured that out.

Let's hope we keep working on that. We have a long way to go to quiet the storms and quell the pollution.

*Many of us do not like dealing with the bad stuff. It's tough enough to keep on course with simply those things that make us happy. Calamities throw us sideways against the wall. We reason that we don't deserve to be inconvenienced or devasted—often by things, we argue, that we can't control. All we want is to be happy and get along. Climate change. Natural disasters. Pandemics. Poverty. Inequity. We simply don't have time to deal with all that. We don't want to deal with any of that. But we must. That's life. That's what happened when sin came into the world. Perfection was gone forever. Nevertheless, we all seek to do and accomplish things that might give us as close to a perfect life as we can achieve. It doesn't happen. Because it can't. That ship sailed a long time ago in the Garden of Eden. We all now live East of Eden, or so John Steinbeck*

tells us.[25] And we do. Our only "out" is to understand that God's grace and mercy through the resurrection of his son, Jesus, can provide end-of-the-day assurances. And peace of mind and heart.

# When Wild Horses Drag You Away

**When I was younger, I used to watch westerns. Admittedly,** they were all pretty much the same. Bad guy wreaks havoc on good guy. Good guy wins in the end.

For some reason, one scene always stuck in my head. It's the one where the guy gets knocked off his horse and his foot gets caught in the stirrup. The horse drags him away until he either falls off or miraculously pulls himself back onto the saddle.

Life is a lot like that scene, particularly if you are the good guy getting constantly beat upon by the bad guy...or constantly being dealt unfortunate circumstances related to health, finances, career, family, enemies, friends who've become enemies, or just bad luck.

I've wondered at times, how many times I can fall or get pushed off that horse and still motivate myself to get back up, particularly when those pushes seem to come in bunches.

A wife dies. A husband dies. A son dies. A daughter dies. A grandchild dies. A friend dies. You lose your job. Your spouse loses a job. You get a frightening health diagnosis. You daughter gets one, too. Your spouse says the marriage is over. Your chief financial officer is embezzling, and your firm is going under. You are arrested for a crime you didn't commit. Or you are arrested for a crime you did commit. Your children won't speak to you. You can't save enough for retirement because things just keep happening that zap what little savings you have. You are retired but realize that you don't have the financial runway to live the way to which you've been accustomed all your life. You become homeless. Your brother becomes homeless. Your son has

151

to be admitted to a mental hospital. Your mother is accused of killing your father. Your daughter is pregnant and doesn't know who the father is. Your son gets someone pregnant but can barely remember her name. You get a flat tire. You return home only to find that the cashier overcharged you. The product you bought to "fix something" doesn't work. You get ready to mow the lawn only to discover you're out of gas. You get in your car to refill the lawnmower cannister only to discover that the car is out of gas, too. Someone rear ends you at a traffic light on the way to a job interview—a job you badly need. A tree falls on your car (yes, the one with no gas) during a storm one night. The special meal you are cooking your spouse because you 'owe her one' burns. The dog eats it, but then throws up so you have to clean that before she arrives home. Your laptop crashes while on deadline for a critical presentation. Your urgent reply gets stuck in outbox, resulting in a missed deadline.

Yes. The list is endless. We seem to constantly be thrown from that wild horse. Sometimes, we simply say "what's the use?" We simply don't want to get back on that horse again.

But we have to.

There was a popular poster hanging on a lot of teenage and college dorm room walls when I was younger. It said, "Not to Decide Is to Decide."

We have a choice. But the consequences of not getting back on that wild horse no matter how wild it might be are far worse than crawling among the rocks beneath its hooves.

We may be bruised. We may be battered. We may have learned a lot. Perhaps we haven't. But there is always hope.

*You cannot possibly read the litany of things gone wrong and not draw a circle around at least one. For some, the circles may be many. We get tired of falling. Sometimes it's self-induced. We make bad choices or decisions. At other times, things just happen. How many times have you thought you've made the perfect call, only for that decision to go south*

*as circumstances change or new information becomes available? You look clearly at the new information and can't do much more than utter, "You've got to be kidding me!" It happens. And sometimes it happens, over and over again. It doesn't seem fair, you say. But life isn't fair. We all come to know that. What keeps us going, keeps us moving forward, is hope. Not the "wishing" kind of hope, but the hope provided us by a higher power, one that assures us in Romans 5: 3-5 that tribulation brings perseverance and perseverance, proven character and proven character, hope. And hope does not disappoint.*

# That Dreaded Question

**We've all had job interviews. During the COVID-19 era** many scrambled to land some of those – interviews as well as jobs.

Interviews are not fun. I've never found them very entertaining—at least not at times when I really needed to nail it. Notice I said "needed." Sometimes, you really need to stick the interview because you really, really need the job. It may not be exactly what you want or pay exactly what you hope, but hey, it's a job. The bills are mounting. Two collections notices arrived just today. You've lost your appetite – which is good because there is nothing in the fridge.

Then there are ones that you really, really "want." The job is exactly what you want to do. It's a great step in your career. The company is great. You'd be working for a well-respected industry leader who would become your mentor. The money is good. The benefits are even better. And well, you just "must" be able to knock the interview out of the park.

And then comes the dreaded question.

"What is your biggest weakness?"

You get a bit fidgety. You feel your heartbeat pick up. Perhaps even get a bit flushed.

"Gosh, I've got to nail this one," you think. "What can I say that makes my weakness look like a strength? Yeah, that's it. I'll use a bit of doublespeak and convince the interviewer that my weakness is not actually a weakness at all, but a strength."

You collect yourself. Sit upright. Push your chest out a little. Move to the front of your chair. And blurt out something like:

"I'm probably too dedicated. I really sink myself into projects and dive into how to solve the problem at hand with all my great co-workers, but sometimes it's at the expense of my personal life. My spouse understands, though, because she only wants what's best for us."

Bells go off in the interviewer's head.

Job and career over family. Good priority. *NOT!*

Bragging about being a team player. *Wasn't this supposed to be about your greatest weakness?*

Being a slave to your job. *So, a life of balance is not important or helpful to you?*

In an effort to show your sense of humor, you come with the clincher.

"I guess, my greatest weakness is thinking I don't have one."

Ding. Ding. Ding. Ding.

While the bells in the interviewer's head have just deafened her, there is a small part of her that at least appreciates the candor, confidence, and self-righteousness.

An interview gone bad.

Okay. Let's admit it. How many of us sometimes think we have such a great grasp of situations and reality that we are bulletproof with no weaknesses?

Many of us are shaking our head.

"Not me," you say. "I realize what a schmuck I am sometimes." But even in our schmuckiness, do we really understand how far we've fallen from grace?

There are none of us with no weaknesses. Most of us understand that. Not all, but most. Even the most confident among us.

There was only one who walked Earth who can claim no weakness. Thankfully, he's the exact one who can provide that grace.

*As unemployment grew during the pandemic then "recalculated" during the road back, I couldn't help thinking about all those who were going through job interviews to get their lives back or to improve their lot in life. Some desperately hoped that the interviewer would grasp onto*

anything they said and like it enough to send them to the next inter-view—or even hire them on the spot. Others, more confident, would use the interviews to showcase themselves. Great skills and attributes. I, too often, would run into the overly confident ones. The ones who for some reason thought they were interviewing "me" and that our firm would be damn lucky to have them. Nothing wrong with a little bit of confidence. But humility and balance go a lot further these days. None of us are without weaknesses—professionally or personally. More of us need to grasp our shortcomings and understand where strength comes from to change. We need to work on that.

# Chipping Away

**Chipping way. Little by Little. That's what's happening.** And it's happening so slowly that few seem to notice. Or care. What am I talking about?

Ever notice how when something new hits the social airways what a big deal it is? Until it's not. Apple phones were novel at a time when the Blackberry reigned. Now everyone has one. In 2008, Tesla debuted its all-electric car, the Roadster, at Detroit's North America International Auto Show. Many smirked and shook their heads. Tesla now sells more than 1,000 EVs a day. The "F" word could not be uttered on TV or in movies. And then it could. Now Green Day spouts it fifty-seven times during a concert and no one seems to notice or care.

When COVID-19 hit mainland USA and began killing thousands a week, the American public could not get enough information about the virus. Media reported around the clock and press conferences became must-see TV. And then they weren't.

Soon the remedies of social distancing, quarantine, masks and washing hands became a pain. It seemed as if the public could only tolerate "abnormal" for a certain period of time. Then it convinced itself that everything really was going to be okay. The curve had flattened, and the virus was going to run its course now that summer and warm weather were approaching. Besides, we needed to get back to work before, God forbid, people started dying of loneliness, jumping off bridges or having heart attacks because of the stress. And yes, economic devastation was taking its toll as well.

The more we are subjected to something, it seems the less we pay attention to it. We simply roll it into our everyday file of "things that I'm going to think less about because I need to move on and keep going."

But where are you going? Have you ever stopped to ask yourself that?

Within a few short months after Covid-19 restrictions began, the Washington Post sent a writer to do a feature article about what reopening was like in a high-end mixed-use retail neighborhood in one of the first states to reopen. At first, the writer's tone was calm and matter of fact. As she observed more and talked to those who had crammed the streets, stores, sidewalks, and restaurants, it was apparent she had stumbled on a very entitled group who, while happy to be free again, were pretty hacked they had been subjected to a lack of normal for several weeks.

One gentleman talked about not being worried at all since he was not in the high-risk race or age group and was in great shape. The reader almost felt as if the man was hoping to get the virus to prove to everyone how inconsequential it was. He no doubt probably thought that once he recovered (should he be so lucky), he was home free, couldn't get it again, couldn't give it to anyone else, and certainly didn't have to follow any of those crazy guidelines anymore. Or so he thought.

Bit by bit, his psyche had been chipped away. He was now able to justify his behavior. I wonder what else he is able to justify. Ageism? Elitism? Racism? Sexism?

How often do we let improprieties chip away at us? How often do we justify the unjustifiable? How often do we make something the norm even though something inside us may throw an alarm?

More often than we care to admit, I suspect. So, good questions on which to end: Where is your heart...and how have you allowed it to be chipped away?

*It's funny that when we don't want to deal with something or be both-ered, we often rationalize it away. Over time, it becomes easier to do.*

We convince ourselves it doesn't exist. Will go away by itself. Someone else will take care of it. Not my problem. I'm good the way I am. All good here! Virus? Pandemic? Racism? Ageism? Sexism? Nah, not me. Not here. Those are just things people conjure up to make others feel guilty and to grind a political or social axe. They are not something I have to deal with. Or want to deal with. I have my life to live, and all that other stuff just gets in my way. So, don't you dare get in my way. Because then I'll fight. Even if I don't understand the cause. Or reality.

# The Great Reveal

**There's this thing going around these days called "The Great Reveal."** Often used to reveal a positive pregnancy result or newly determined sex of the baby. Some of them have been pretty clever. Love the ones *The Today Show* shares from time to time.

Sometimes the great reveal is not always what we hope for, though. Particularly when it results in the discovery of an underlying prejudice. That we doggedly try to dismiss.

I'd love to say that I'm color blind and that there is not a prejudiced bone in my body. But I know I'd be lying. We all have prejudices. We just choose to sweep them to the far corners of our mind. Refuse to admit them or deal with them.

It's more comfortable for us that way.

When we discover them, though, we need to admit them—at least to ourselves—and then commit to work on them. Understand why they exist. Find ways to change our thinking. Interact with those who perhaps make us a bit uncomfortable.

Let me give you an example.

The other day I called the local deli to place a special order. The deli asked when I wanted to pick it up. I gave a time. It said fine.

Knowing *my* time is not always *its* time, I called back to confirm close to the time I'd requested.

I was transferred to the deli department and was greeted less than warmly by an accent I didn't recognize and barely understood. I asked if this was the deli. I was told rather curtly—or so I perceived—that it was.

I shared my name and asked if my order was ready. There was a long pause.

"Hello! Is anyone there?" I asked in a rather loud voice. I was in a hurry. I didn't want to drive to the deli if I would have to wait.

The accented response came back and again asked for my name. I told him AGAIN. Another long pause. He then asked AGAIN about the order I had placed. I told him AGAIN.

By now I was getting nowhere. I was agitated. I'm thinking, "For Pete's sake. I called early. Re-called to confirm. Provided my name a dozen times (not really) to confirm the same order and some idiot on the other end of the phone is obviously clueless and can't get it straight."

I AGAIN asked even more tersely whether my order was ready.

Another long pause.

With an accent barely discernable, I heard, "Yes, it is." Then a click. That was it.

I was ticked. How rude! Is that any way to treat your customers? Especially one that comes in there all the time. I'm a loyal client. You can't treat me like that. I'll just take my business and order somewhere else next time. You know, you're not the only deli around!

Then I began to calm down. I began to think, "What just happened here?"

I heard an accent that was different, difficult to understand. I became irritable because my inability to understand that accent was keeping me from communicating the way *I* wanted and to get the answer *I* wanted.

I began to think about the voice—and the PERSON—on the other end of that phone line. He was definitely an immigrant. I wondered how long he had lived in the area, how long he had even lived in the US. I wondered where he had come from. What were conditions like in his previous country? I wondered how difficult it was to get here. Become accepted. If he even felt welcomed and accepted . How difficult it had been to learn the language, to get the job at the deli? Was he overqualified for it? Perhaps it was all he could find to support his family. I wondered about his family. Where did they live? What type of housing? Were they able make ends meet with just his deli job?

I thought about how I reacted and perceived his English as curt. I took a breath and then tried to understand not only how difficult it is to learn English in the first place, but how even harder it is learn all the tone inflections, correct syllable emphasis, and even facial expressions that must accompany that newly learned language for us long-time American residents to find his communication acceptable and gratifying to our ears.

I was embarrassed. Unconsciously, I had actually committed the sin of exclusion and non-acceptance that I so often rail against.

I must do better.

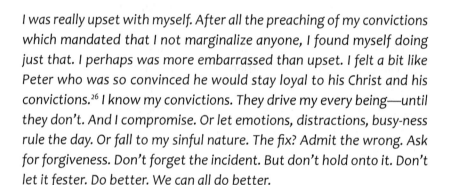

*I was really upset with myself. After all the preaching of my convictions which mandated that I not marginalize anyone, I found myself doing just that. I perhaps was more embarrassed than upset. I felt a bit like Peter who was so convinced he would stay loyal to his Christ and his convictions.[26] I know my convictions. They drive my every being—until they don't. And I compromise. Or let emotions, distractions, busy-ness rule the day. Or fall to my sinful nature. The fix? Admit the wrong. Ask for forgiveness. Don't forget the incident. But don't hold onto it. Don't let it fester. Do better. We can all do better.*

# Ch-Ch-Ch-Ch-Changes

**For the last 20 years or so I have valued change. You** know, the kind the cashier gives you. For the entire year, I put it in a glass jar. Then I continue a tradition.

Each Christmas, I find some sort of interesting container, dump the change into it, and send it to my daughter. One year, it was a pair of socks for her fiancé.

When she was little, she thought it was fun to separate all the coins by denomination and place them into coin rolls before taking them to the bank to see how much money she had to spend.

As she got older, she tired of the coin rolls and just found a machine that separated them for her. One year, as she moved into adulthood, she asked me why I did that and how long was I going to continue.

I told her it was inevitable that she would have change long after I was gone. She looked at me quizzically. I explained:

"As has become our tradition (one of which I hope you never tire), I am sending you all the loose change I have saved during the year. I know. It's never very much. But that's not the point. The point is actually three-fold.

"One, every time I come home at the end of the day and put those coins in the jar, I think of you. So, know that not a day goes by that I don't think of you.

"Two, it is in the spirit of giving. I wish I could give you so much more, but if there's one thing I hope I have ingrained in you, it is the spirit and desire to give. There is no greater joy than giving.

"Third, it is all about change, and not the literal coinage kind. Each and every day, we should ask ourselves what we can do to change

163

things and make the world better. The world doesn't change unless we do our part; and Lord knows, there is much change needed."

One of my favorite expressions is "If nothing changes ... then nothing ever changes." Think about it. Status quo is never acceptable. We can always do better. Don't settle. Change things. Be a crusader. Be an advocate. Find causes and ways to become involved. Have a voice. Be a voice.

At no time is that more necessary than now as we see so much crumbling around us. So many of us see change as a huge mountain and think of ourselves as inconsequential or too small a piece to make a difference. Not so. Each small step up that mountain gets us closer to the top.

Sometimes, we just don't know what to do. We need the push, the help of another. Sometimes it must be us reaching back to pull someone struggling along.

At one point in my life, I spent several years asking God to use me. Show me how to serve. Show me where to serve. Show me how to cause change. I got so frustrated. No answers seemed to come while time was wasting away. I even began to pray for the bolt of lightning or a dream in the middle of the night.

Then one very quiet morning, I got an answer. And it was not quite what I expected.

"Ya' know, I've got my hands pretty full right now. This is an evil and destructive world. And while I love you, and watch over you each and every day, you need to do some of the heavy lifting yourself every once in a while. Just do *something*. I have given you a brain. I have given you a heart. I have provided you with intelligence and wisdom and compassion. Use them...and just do *something*. Trust me. I'll tap you on the shoulder if you are going down the wrong path."

The time has come where silence isn't good enough. It's time to change things. It's time to do...*something*.

I hope my daughter is a faster learner than I am. I hope she continues the tradition.

———————∝———————

*The older I get, the more I realize I am one day closer to not being here any longer. I realize I have lived more years than I have remaining. Have I used my talents and gifts the way God intended me to use them? I've certainly screwed up a bunch. An easy admission. But I also know that God's not done with me yet. So, what does that mean? Change. I know there are things I can do to affect change. Some are small. Some are not so small. What are they? I want to be sure that I'm doing the right things. Not wasting time doing the less significant things. Doing what God wants me to do. So, God, tell me what that is. Or so was the question I asked for a number of years. I was anxious. When God answered my prayer, he removed the anxiety. And replaced it with eagerness. "Just do something. I'll let you know if you're heading down the right path or not." Sometimes small. Sometimes significant. I quit asking for the lightning bolt, dream or ah-ha moment. And jumped in. Sure, it's been a bit messy at times. But now, my smile is bigger than it's ever been, and I really, really sleep well at night. Just do something.*

# Recognize, Decide, Do

**How many of you have had an a-ha moment? They hit** when we least expect it. Middle of the night. Driving. Listening to a song. Perhaps even while driving in the middle of the night listening to a song.

My most recent a-ha moment came during a Zoom meeting earlier this summer. Granted, the summer has been a rough one. We all know what I'm talking about. No need to belabor.

But there I was, early one Friday, morning listening to a four-person panel, socially distanced on a stage, all trying to bring some clarity to what everyone knew was not normal.

Orchestrated by an inner city non-profit, the panel featured a former president of an historically Black college, an executive from a faith-based organization, an executive director of an educational center for wayward youth, and a student who regularly attended the center.

The questions went back and forth.

The young man shared, "You can't tell a dog how to bark when he's been locked in a cage a hundred days." Translation: Don't tell someone how they are *supposed* to act or what they are *supposed* to say or how they are *supposed* to react when you've restricted them for such a long period of time. You're not going to get a thank you and a smile.

Pretty insightful words from a 16-year-old. The faith-based exec provided even more clarity.

His thoughts? At times like this, it's imperative we **recognize** that things need to change. But recognition isn't enough. I think most all understand that. We must **decide** that something needs to be done to fix things. But that still isn't enough. All too many of us sit around, recognize the problem, and see a way to bring change. But recognizing and deciding are not enough. We must actually **do** something about it. Not talk about it. Not hope that others draw the same conclusion and do it. We ourselves must decide to DO.

For each one of us, that could be something different. Provide financial help. March. Become mentors. Provide vocal and emotional support to those on the front lines. Step up to the front lines. Do something we didn't think we were capable of doing. (Makes me think of Philippians 4:13.)

But DO something.

The a-ha moment came in the form of a tee-shirt fund-raising campaign. The educational center accepted the challenge and created tee-shirts that said RECOGNIZE-DECIDE-DO on the front (with its name on the back). The crowdfunding campaign sent a tee-shirt to anyone who contributed $50 or more. All funds went to the center that works with economically and educationally challenged kids, many of whom have had at least one not-so-fabulous experience with the police.

The center's programming is working. Only 4 percent of its student members have a second offense versus the norm of 70 percent.

The campaign raised several thousand dollars for the educational center. And the tee-shirts were really cool.

*The interesting lesson here is that the wisdom originated from a 16-year-old. His mentor put it into perspective. So often, we use our life experiences to "deep think" how to handle something. Afterall, we've had all these life experiences. We may as well put them to use to figure things out. Some use their educational degrees. Some, their years on the job or of service. Some the great self-help book they've just read. But sitting on the stage that day was a man who just nailed it. Recognize that something is wrong (i.e., racial/social injustice, poverty, educational inadequacies). Decide something needs to be done. And then don't wait around for someone else to do it. Jump in. And do it.*

# Pass

**It was fall. The leaves had yet to turn. But there was a** cool, crispness to the air. The kind of day where you either throw on shorts and a sweatshirt or jeans and a tee-shirt.

He opted for the latter, sporting one of his advocacy tee-shirts. The men sat in a circle in front of the fireplace at the clubhouse. After some initial good-natured jostling of whose college team had crushed another's that weekend, talk turned to blessings and prayer requests.

An elderly parent. A son looking for a new job. An expecting daughter with complications. Upcoming travel. A business dilemma. An onery co-worker. Home repairs. Financial concerns. The upcoming election.

The request queue came closer. The man to his right prayed for healing for his dog. It was up there in years and such a part of the family. The man closed with salutatory "woof." Now, it was his turn. There was much on his heart. Silence. A full minute passed. Some of the men began to squirm and shuffle.

"Pass," he uttered.

More silence before the next began and the leader finally closed.

Discussion began on how to be better neighbors. Literally. Within our community. How we could help each other. How we could share God's love to those around us. How we could get friends and colleagues to come to our church and become involved. Corporate worship. One grows with corporate worship and by doing projects with our fellow parishioners.

Finally, it was time to close in prayer. The leader asked for a volunteer. The until-now-silent man raised his hand. Heads bowed.

"Lord, forgive us for our infidelities and lack of understanding. Forgive us for not recognizing injustice and prejudice. Forgive us for not understanding the marginalized and recognizing that their needs are different than ours. Forgive us for only reaching out to those who look like us. Forgive us for only worshiping and congregating with those who look like us and want the same things we do. Forgive us for being comfortable enough to share with each other, but not comfortable enough to go into areas of the city where we are in the minority and feel intimidated. Forgive us for not trying to understand the plight of those who don't live like us and worship where we do. Forgive us for not understanding that we have so much, and others have so little. Forgive us for being comfortable. Allow us to see difficult situations with others as opportunities and not challenges we are unequipped to handle. Change our hearts to understand the needs of the least of these, our brothers, as they face social and racial injustices we could never imagine...Amen."

Bowed heads raised. Little was said.

*While God wants us and instructs us to bring him all our concerns, I sometimes think he shakes his head and says, "Really?!" He knows our needs. Or at least that's what the scriptures tell us. But I sometimes think He needs to know our heart for those who don't have -- but need.*

# Faulty Glasses

**Those of us with sight take much for granted.**

We climb out of bed at various times. Some long before the chickens wake. Some as the sun rises. Some around lunch time. Not sure I get that last one, but I know there are many people whose jobs (or play) may not bring them home until the wee hours. So, a bit different perspective.

The first thing we do, usually, when our feet hit the floor is open our eyes. You may flick on a light. You may not. You may stumble to the bathroom, kitchen or dog dish with still foggy vision. But eventually, things become clear. Or at least you think.

I once read that baseball's Ted Williams, perhaps the greatest hitter of all time, had 20/10 vision. In addition to understanding the mechanics of hitting a baseball and having a near flawless swing, he saw practically every stitch of the baseball from the pitcher's hand to his bat.

I envied Ted Williams. I was a pretty good hitter, but there was plenty I didn't see as well as I wished. Particularly that 95-mph fastball. The breaking pitch? The curve? I actually handled them okay. Perhaps there's a life metaphor there somewhere.

Many begin to have vision issues when they approach middle age. Some earlier. Some upon birth. Some don't see colors very distinctly. Some can't see at all.

And some people walk through life with perpetually clouded vision. They've tried glasses— reading and prescription. They've progressed from 2.0 to 3.25 reading glasses. Eye disease. Eye surgery.

Some choose rose-colored glasses. Others seem to peer continually through cracked lenses. I'm obviously not talking about eyesight now.

Perspective.

I've never quite grasped how two people can look directly at the same thing, and see it differently, even describe it differently. Same goes for listening. Why do some people hear the same words one way, while another, another way? Why do your spouse or kids hear or see something one way, when you mean something entirely different? Why do Republicans and Democrats see issues surrounding the economy, race, education, guns, environment, equality differently? Through what lens are they looking?

Why do some people believe there is a God? Others not so much. Or at all. What do some people see? What do others not see?

While I'm neither an ophthalmologist nor neurologist, I suspect that one trained as such would tell you that we really don't see with our eyes. We see with our brain. It processes what we see. And how we see it.

While color or lack thereof may be the first sensory reaction, we see far deeper as a result of exposure and experiences. We see what we want to see sometimes (okay, most of the time) because to do otherwise, is uncomfortable. We detest lack of comfort. We hate being wrong.

It's easy to blame those faulty glasses, faulty lenses. But perhaps we need to concentrate a bit more on our heart rather than our eyes and our brain to be sure we get it right— whatever right may mean in your world. Which may be the heart of the problem.

So how do we fix faulty vision?

*Most get the metaphor. Generations from now, people will look back on the pandemic and shake their heads at the millions who refused to accept God's science. Some even believed it to be a hoax as they lay gasping their final breath minutes from the casket. There was an insurrection against democracy, and yet some politicians and their followers referred to it as a gentle visitation. There was election ballot verification confirmed repeatedly, yet some claimed foul and went out of their*

way to create controversy and dissension. Others refused to believe data on environmental calamities reported virtually every day and projected long range.

God gave humans a brain far more sophisticated than any other being on earth. Yet to me, it's obvious that the brain doesn't work very well sometimes. I defer to the heart, hoping that man can see suffering and inequities and chose to change them. But even the heart gets hardened along the way sometimes. As divisiveness ruled on a wide variety of issues, it became apparent to me that trying to rationalize with someone whose opinion was different than mine was futile. I could lay out all the facts and verifiable data from non-biased sources, but I never was going to get a response of, "Oh, my gosh. You're right. I can't believe I've been so blind and stupid." Wasn't going to happen. The only one who can change minds and hearts is God. So that's where I try to focus. How does God, specifically Christ in the New Testament, tell us we should handle lack of clarity, pushback? I keep praying.

# The Dinner Party

**It was a well-kept inner-city neighborhood of stately** townhomes. We had been invited to a dinner party. No special cause. The hosts simply wanted to share an epicurean evening with close friends. Malachi answered the doorbell. Gave me a big hug. A gracious bow to my wife.

He welcomed us and took us to meet several other guests who had already arrived. The discussion was already lively. Kelli told us to jump right in. They were discussing a recent zoning change that was to bring a large corporation to the neighborhood. Some claimed the corporation was necessary to provide jobs and enhance the neighborhood's tax base. Others said it would continue to escalate real estate costs and push out those in the neighborhood who were having a hard time holding onto their legacy properties. One argument was that it allowed those legacy owners to sell and take the money and run to a better area to live. Others railed against displacing the more impoverished in the community for the sake of progress.

Wanda summoned us over to their discussion. She wanted to invite us to their church that Sunday. An esteemed international scholar would be dissecting the Book of Acts and what it meant for today's culture and society.

Wine was poured. Appetizers shared. Jokes told.

"Did you hear the one about the local preacher who had to descend from heaven?" asked Jamison.

"No, what happened?"

"Seems he ran out of chalk and had to get some more in order to write all his indiscretions on Life's blackboard."

"Man, there might not be enough chalk for me," laughed another.

Finally, dinner was set. All gathered around the well-appointed table setting. Hands held. Malachi asked the blessing.

A week later, we headed to our next dinner invitation. The colonial brick sat at the rear of the cul-de-sac. The lawn perfectly manicured. The John Deere had done a masterful job.

We were the last to arrive. We could hear the raucous crowd inside. We knocked. No one answered, so we opened the door and walked in.

It was a while before anyone knew another couple had arrived. But that's because the perennial southern college behemoth had just scored on a trick play.

Billy shoved a beer into my hand. My wife found her way to the kitchen with her prepared "side dish" for the evening.

The gathering was getting louder and louder with each series, the commentators dissecting every play. Skeptics in the room took exception to the analysis.

The guys gravitated to the big screen. The gals gathered in the kitchen.

"Hey, how's your golf game?" Randy asked.

"Don't play anymore," I answered. "No time. Too busy saving the world," I smiled.

"Well, when you change your mind, let me know. I have a standing Sunday morning tee time at the club."

"Have you eaten at any great new restaurants lately," Karen asked my wife, who shared that we really hadn't.

"Well, tell me all about the next trip you two have planned," she continued.

Without awaiting an answer, she effused, "We're going to Tuscany next month. We're so excited. We did Southern France two years ago, but we've heard Tuscany is even better. Can't wait to learn all about those wines and great foods. We'll probably come back ten pounds heavier and with a sore liver."

She laughed uncontrollably awaiting a response...from anyone.

"We're going to Greenville next weekend," my wife offered.

"Oh, (pause) that sounds nice," came the reply. "Do you have relatives there?"

"No, we just think it's a charming city. We can relax there."

As halftime arrived, everyone was told to grab a plate and find a place to sit. The back porch was an option as was the living room, screened in porch, or dining area.

"Dig in," announced Randy. "The second half begins in fifteen minutes."

"Quite a contrast," my wife uttered on the way home.

"Yes," I agreed. "Kinda like the difference between black and white."

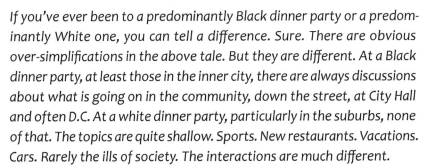

*If you've ever been to a predominantly Black dinner party or a predominantly White one, you can tell a difference. Sure. There are obvious over-simplifications in the above tale. But they are different. At a Black dinner party, at least those in the inner city, there are always discussions about what is going on in the community, down the street, at City Hall and often D.C. At a white dinner party, particularly in the suburbs, none of that. The topics are quite shallow. Sports. New restaurants. Vacations. Cars. Rarely the ills of society. The interactions are much different.*

*In this story, the (White) couple is met warmly at the door of the Black party by the host, shown in and introduced to the others who are in deep discussion over many of the day's issues. The White party is a free-for-all. No one answers the door. The couple is barely recognized when they enter. The host finally shoves a beer into the guy's hand while allowing his wife to wander aimlessly to the kitchen to find a spot for what she has brought to the dinner. The guys watch the football game. The women gather in the kitchen. When it's time for dinner, the Black dinner party says grace and all sit around a large table. At the White dinner party, it's every man and women for themselves to find a spot in one of four areas suitable.*

*Okay, yes. I've been to Black dinner cookouts where football was the key topic. But there still was a lot more discussion about world* events—and religion. And I've been to White dinner parties when politics came up. Those discussions usually ended badly.

I've come to the conclusion that the best dinner parties include Jesus, a beer, and a cigar.

# Man in the Crowd

*I read a lot. I've already professed to that. Sometimes I read something so profound or moving that I simply have to share. This is one of those. It is an incredible thought for everyday living. The text is from Pulitzer Prize winner Isabel Wilkerson's "Caste—The Origins of Our Discontent."*

There is a famous black-and-white photograph from the era of the Third Reich. It is a picture taken in Hamburg, Germany, in 1936, of shipyard workers, a hundred or more, facing the same direction in the light of the sun. They are heiling in unison, their right arms rigid in outstretched allegiance to the Fuhrer.

If you look closely, you can see a man in the upper right who is different from the others. His face is gentle but unyielding. Modern-day displays of the photograph will often add a helpful red circle around the man or an arrow pointing to him. He is surrounded by fellow citizens caught under the spell of Nazis. He keeps his arms folded to his chest, as the stiff palms of the others hover just inches from him. He alone is refusing to salute. He is the one man standing against the tide.

Looking back from our vantage point, he is the only person in the entire scene who is on the right side of history. Everyone around him is tragically, fatefully, categorically wrong. In that moment, only he could see it.

His name is believed to have been August Landmesser. At this time, he could not have known the murderous path the hysteria around him would lead to. But he had already seen enough to reject it.

He had joined the Nazi Party himself years before. By now though, he knew firsthand that the Nazis were feeding Germans lies about the Jews, the outcastes of his era, that, even this early in the Reich, the

Nazis had caused terror, heartache and disruption. He knew that Jews were anything but *Untermenschen,* that they were German citizens, human as anyone else. He was an Aryan in love with a Jewish woman, but the recently enacted Nuremburg Laws had made their relationship illegal. They were forbidden to marry or have sexual relations, either of which amounted to what the Nazis called "racial infamy."

His personal experience and close connection to the scapegoated caste allowed him to see past the lies and the stereotypes so readily embraced by susceptible members—the majority, sadly—of the dominant caste. Though Aryan himself, his openness to the humanity of the people who had been deemed beneath him gave him a stake in their well-being, their fates tied to his. He could see what his countrymen chose not to see.

In a totalitarian regime such as that of the Third Reich, it was an act of bravery to stand firm against an ocean. We would all want to believe that we would have been him. We might feel certain that, were we Aryan citizens under the Third Reich, we surely would have seen through it, would have risen above it like him, been that person resisting authoritarianism and brutality in the face of mass hysteria.

We would like to believe that we would have taken the more difficult path of standing up against injustice in defense of the outcaste. But unless people are willing to transcend their fears, endure discomfort and derision, suffer the scorn of loved ones and neighbors and co-workers and friends, fall into disfavor of perhaps everyone they know, face exclusion and even banishment, it would be numerically impossible, humanly impossible, for everyone to be that man. What would it take to be him in any era? What would it take to be him now?[27]

(With thanks to Isabel Wilkerson)

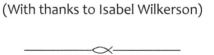

*There are three books that I point to as life-changing reads. One is Rick Warren's "A Purpose Driven Life." Another, John Ortberg's "If You Want to Walk on Water You Have to Get Out of the Boat."[28] And then*

Isabel Wilkerson's "Caste." If one wants an understanding of how races evolved and why, no better book has ever been written. The Pulitzer Prize winning Wilkerson describes with incredible data and accuracy the ascent of systemic racism from the time the first Black men and women landed on America's shores until today. It's a thick book. But hard to put down. I tell people, if nothing else, read Chapters 8 and 9. They were truly "Holy Smokes" moments for me. I began to understand.

# SPORTS & ENTERTAINMENT

# The Hammer

**I pulled the broom handle from the closet and grabbed** a sheet of tin foil. I wadded it into a ball and went out the backdoor into my field of dreams. I lived in the country, so my number one play-mate was me.

But that was okay. I'd scratched out a baseball diamond in my backyard, and that day, with all my imaginary players and fans, it was the World Series. Game Seven. At least in my own little world.

My teams were the Atlanta Braves and the New York Yankees. All my school buddies loved the Yankees. What was there not to like? The Yanks had been to five Series that decade and won two. I was a Braves guy.

And this was my imagination. My teams were my teams. And if I wanted the Braves to be playing the Yankees, then the Braves would be playing the Yankees. In Game Seven.

I enacted every pitch. Every batter. Every cheer of the crowd for nine innings. I ran the bases. Slid into a shortstop to break up a double play. Bowled over a catcher to score a go-ahead run.

But now it was the bottom of the ninth. The Braves had lost their lead and were down 7-4. Hank Aaron was scheduled to bat sixth that inning. If we could just get to The Hammer.

As luck would have it, the Braves loaded the bases. Two outs. And Henry came to the plate. The announcers were at a crescendo pitch. The fans were breaking decibels. My dog was barking.

Ball one. Ball two. Hank had him just where he wanted him. A nasty breaking pitch. Strike one. An off-speed pitch. Strike two. Next pitch, barely outside. Ball three.

Full count. Bases loaded. Braves down 7-4. Last inning. Game Seven. World Series.

"And there's the wind up," the announcer in me shouted, "and the pitch..."

Thwack!

"There's a long fly ball to deep center field. Mantle is going back. Back. Back...It's GONE!...Hank Aaron has done it. The Braves have won the World Series." I had simply crushed that foil ball.

As I rounded the base at third, I couldn't help but think about how great it must be to be Hank Aaron.

Little boys grow up.

I went to college to play baseball. I came South. I eventually wanted to end up in Atlanta. Like Hank. I was actually watching April 8, 1974 on a small black and white TV in my college apartment when Hank hit home run 715 to break the Babe's record. I'm sure many of us remember where we were when he hit the shot heard round the world.

It was a brave shot. Not so much because of its position in sports history—oh sure, that will remain legendary—but more for its symbolism of what it meant for civil rights.

For you see, so much hate and anger followed Aaron. From his roots in Mobile, AL to the Indianapolis Clowns of the Negro League then to the Braves via Boston and Milwaukee. Letters. Death threats. Hotel capers to keep him safe.

Through it all, he remained undeterred. He knew he was given a gift. We all knew he was given a gift. Most of us thought it was to play baseball as well as anyone who had ever played the game.

But his real gift was his grace. Grace, oft defined as simple elegance or refinement of movement; courteous, goodwill. Hank Aaron was all of those.

There was a certain divine grace to Henry as well - an influence that gave humans the ability to regenerate and inspire virtuous impulses while imparting strength to endure trial and resist the temptation to strike back.

Aaron's legacy as one of Atlanta's great civil rights icons may surpass even his on-field exploits. In the City Too Busy to Hate, they all looked up to him. Martin Luther King, Jr., Andy Young, John Lewis, Joseph Lowrey, C.T. Vivian, Hosea Williams, Vernon Jordan - and the list goes on.

I never made it past college ball. But I did make it to Atlanta. For that I am grateful. To see Aaron play. To see Aaron live. And to remember him hitting that Game Seven grand slam in my backyard.

*Hank Aaron died unexpectedly January 22, 2021. Henry was the bravest of the Braves, undergoing unimaginable racist treatment during a time when he should have been exulted as one of the greatest of his generation—not only for his on-field feats but even more for his community and philanthropic efforts.*

*This was written shortly after Hank's funeral. I couldn't help but reach back into the far recesses of my childhood and remember my games in the backyard where Hank and other players of color usually stole the show, exciting the dreams of a young boy who one day hoped to play on the same diamonds as Hank. Bob Gibson. Juan Marichal. Roberto Clemente. Jim Mudcat Grant. Willie Mays. Dick Allen. Curt Flood. Lou Brock. Maury Wills. I could go on and on.*

*Those were the happiest days of my life. Carefree. On a make-shift baseball field. Without a care in the world except who would be that day's hero.*

*Hank Aaron was a hero for so many—on the field and off. We will miss him.*

# Go Brave!

**I love the fall. Weather is spectacular. My only child was** born then. Football returns. And of course, the Major League Baseball playoffs begin, culminating in a World Series.

I have long been a Braves fan going back to their days in Milwaukee. When they moved to Atlanta, I thought, "Wow, Atlanta must be a pretty cool place if my Braves are moving there."

As a result, I came south to play baseball in college. I have lived in Atlanta most of my adult life. Have experienced "Worst to First," fourteen consecutive division titles, a World Series Championship (should have been more), and a recent resurgence that has had us in the playoffs the last several years.

I begin each year thinking this could be our year. Who knows? Maybe.

But there is one thing that isn't quite right with the Braves. Its name. The Native American community finds the moniker a bit unsettling. Sure, certain Native American groups give the team lip service, but wouldn't you if your casinos were a major promotional partner of the team? In talking with Native American groups, I'm told some simply hold their noses while others adamantly want change.

So, what gives? In an era where racial groups fight denigration, when will the time come that the Braves understand they must make a change? And when that happens, what will that change be?

I shared an idea with a columnist. He printed it. And a movement began. Albeit, a subtle movement. Quiet support grew among Atlanta corporate, civil rights and community leaders to encourage a very slight but poignant tweak. The Atlanta BRAVE.

Gee, that doesn't seem like enough of a change to make a difference, you say. So why all the support?

Atlanta understands its unique place in history as the cradle of the civil rights movement. Brave leaders at a critical time of our nation. Martin Luther King, Jr., Coretta Scott King, John Lewis, Ralph David Abernathy, Andy Young, C.T Vivian, Joseph Lowery, Vernon Jordan and countless others.

That courage and leadership is not restricted just to the Black community, however. Brave leadership has come from the likes of Mayor Ivan Allen, former President Jimmy Carter, Olympics chieftain Billy Payne, media mogul Ted Turner and a host of dream changers.

Just picture an Atlanta BRAVE organization that continues to honor leadership, bravery, and contributions within the Native American community, while creating a Wall of Fame to honor brave Georgians, Atlantans and Native Americans.

It seems like a rebranding with a generous endorsement of that branding from an enthusiastic and supportive corporate and civic community, could go a long way to heal some of the pandemic era financial wounds not to mention racial ones.

What a great story to share with the league and nation about how the local team realized its impact on the City Too Busy to Hate.

> "Our nation was born in genocide when it embraced the doctrine that the original American, the Indian, was an inferior race. Even before there were large numbers of Negroes on our shores, the scar of racial hatred had already disfigured colonial society. From the sixteenth century forward, blood flowed in battles of racial supremacy. We are perhaps the only nation which tried as a matter of national policy to wipe out its indigenous population. Moreover, we elevated that tragic experience into a noble crusade. Indeed, even today we have not permitted ourselves to reject or to feel remorse for this shameful episode. Our literature, our films, our drama, our folklore all exalt it."[29]

> – Rev. Dr. Martin Luther King, Jr.

———————⟨⟨⟩⟩———————

*This is a no-brainer. Talk about unification and harmony! Talk about uniting all the races via the courage, leadership and bravery of not only our indigenous Americans, but those who helped make the City of Atlanta the great city it has become, the City Too Busy to Hate. Many have called this small tweak an "elegant solution." Yet others dig in resistant to change and even label it "woke" or "political grandstanding." After all, they say, there is nothing offensive about "Braves." Yes, bravery is honorable. But that's not what the moniker represents. It represents an indigenous American population that was murdered, denigrated and relocated to make way for the White man. The right thing would be to honor true bravery, contributions and leadership. The Brave.*

[Note: The Atlanta Braves won the World Series in 2021, while the Native American community continued to urge change.]

# Game, Set, Match

**A friendly game of mixed doubles.**

Well, actually it was more than that. It was the club championship. Several days of long, tortuous sets. In the heat. Rain delays. Cramps. Blisters. Questionable line calls.

And then there was the bunting. The flags. The loud speaker. The fans in the stands. All for a community club championship.

Whew. This was serious.

John and Lisa were the newcomers. They had moved south from the Cape a year ago, wanting to be near their daughter. She was in medical school at the prestigious southern university. Both were good, although squarely set in middle age. Collegiate stars. Lisa had won an NCAA singles title years ago. That's where she caught John's eye. They were a team almost since day one and had won many a club championship—and a few regional tourneys along the way over the last twenty-plus years.

Andy and Andrea (known as Andy-squared to their friends) were the defending champions. Younger. Risk takers. A tad flashy. Showmen. The club members loved it.

A-squared won the coin flip. The crowd whistled and cheered. They elected to serve first.

"Let's go for the jugular early," Andrea whispered to Andy.

Andy crushed his first serve. Ace. John moved to the other side of the court for Andy's next serve. This time, John blasted it back down the line past Andrea. Andy gave her the "why didn't you cover that" look. Andrea rolled her eyes.

Back and forth it went. The first set reached deuce six times. John then returned another scorcher by Andrea whom he found poaching.

During the next long volley, Lisa took a huge hit from Andy at the net and back-handed it hard by Andrea. The newbies had broken serve on the first game.

As they trade sides, Andy chided his mate for what he called erratic play.

"If we're going to go for the jugular, we both have to do our part," he said.

Andrea raised her eyebrows and took her spot on the end line. Lisa was serving.

Back and forth it went. The passing shot to Andrea's backhand side seemed to be there repeatedly. When she tried to cheat, Andy was left scrambling to cover more court than he was capable.

John and Lisa were on the same page. They talked. They strategized. They played mind games with their opponents.

Once, with Andy serving and seeming to lose serve as the ball barely edged outside the line, John called the ball in to bring the score back to deuce and give Andy more life. Two serves later, it was John and Lisa's game. It was like, "I'm going to show you that I can beat you even after giving you a break, because I'm that much better than you today."

It wasn't a cocky thing. It was mind manipulation. Lisa knew exactly what her husband was doing. She was on the same page. They were a team. And they were very good at being teammates.

John and Lisa won in straight sets. The defending champions had been beaten. Easily.

As the couple shook hands, Andy muttered something about not believing he and Andrea had lost to "the old guys."

"There are certain things that come with age," smiled Lisa. "Great wines...and great communication. We'll send you over a bottle of our finest this evening to soothe your wounds. The communication you're going to have to work on yourself."

The defending champs had learned a lesson that day.

---—⋈—---

*The greatest attribute a couple can have is communication. It isn't easy. It takes time. It takes a willingness to learn. A willingness to compromise. A willingness to overlook some things, stand firm on others. It's about respecting each other and listening to each other. My spouse and I are very different. She's quiet and reserved. I'm a bit more excitable and driven. She grounds me when I go over the top. Not by challenging me, but by asking questions for which I honestly have no good answer. There are times when she knows it's okay to let me rant, because I just need to get it out of my system before I get back to normal. And all is right with the world again. But it's taken a while to learn how to communicate.*

*The younger couple above was brash, confident and assertive. Not totally abominable characteristics if controlled properly. But they were still learning. The older couple had figured much of it out. Their communication had come with age as had their wisdom. The younger couple could not fathom losing to communication and wisdom...because they didn't have it and weren't able to recognize it. Perhaps, over that bottle of wine, they learned something from the gracious communicators.*

# On Bended Knee

**I continue to read article after article, opinion after** opinion from those who don't believe athletes should be commended or listened to for their social viewpoints.

Honestly, I'm more than a bit tired of hearing people rail on athletes calling them spoiled, brain dead, clueless and spotlight seekers.

In case you haven't noticed or just landed from another galaxy, this country is in pretty bad shape right now. Country? Heck, the entire planet. Worldwide pandemic, economic, racial, educational, healthcare, environmental, and insurrection woes are rampant.

We are witnessing racial unrest unlike that seen since the 1960's. The killing of George Floyd after countless others was a significant lynch pin. Now Black people and other minorities are screaming for racial, social, economic, healthcare and education equality. Some say they are screaming too loudly. Some accuse them of promoting violence over protest. Some of those accusers wouldn't know the difference.

Many of the candidly outspoken voices of injustice have been professional athletes and coaches like LeBron James, Gregg Popovich, Steve Kerr, Maya Moore, Serena Williams, Aly Raisman, Bubba Wallace, Lloyd Pierce, Malcolm Brogdan, Ty Dillon, Patrick Mahomes, Saquon Barkley, Michael Thomas, and many, many others. Those speaking out have become a pretty long and formidable list.

To those who are telling these athletes to just shut up and play, I ask, "to whom are you looking to lead this movement from depravity and injustice?" Or don't you even want to acknowledge it exists?

Unlike the 60's when it was easy to identify leaders like Martin Luther King, Jr., John Lewis, Ralph David Abernathy, Andrew Young, and Robert Kennedy as they called out injustice, to whom are you looking now? Or do you feel (and hope) that everything will quiet down and quell after contentious elections, and we'll get back to normal with a flourishing economy (for whom?) and sound health-care (really?!)?

Not going to happen. We are in a new and unique era. It is the era of social media and, like it or not, those with the biggest pulpit are those with the biggest social platform and following. Many of those are our sports stars. So, be thankful that many of these socially con-scious, educated, street-savvy soldiers whose traits exude leadership on the playing field have decided to take their leadership skills into the community.

Not only are they able to contribute financially, but they are able to rally and assemble large coalitions for change through their lead-ership, viewpoints, and social media channels.

Don't like social media rants? Neither do I sometimes. But that horse has left the barn.

Don't agree with their viewpoints? Ah, that may be part of the problem. Perhaps you don't agree with their right to even speak up and be heard as well. Shame. I believe those patriotic symbols to which you point and wholeheartedly believe such as the flag, the Constitution, and the Statue of Liberty give them every right to do exactly that. They *are* exercising their patriotism by taking a stand against injustice.

And you know what? If the majority of Americans don't believe in the message, it won't resonate. Those athlete voices will become less powerful, less impactful, less influential and the message and movement will die. That's how it works.

But you know what? That's not happening.

And don't think it's just Black athletes crying out. Sure, White people/athletes don't understand what they can't understand, but there are many who want to learn and stand with their Black and Brown and Yellow and Red brothers.

You find many taking a knee to support racial injustice and Black Lives Matter (yes, all lives matter, but until one can admit that Black

Lives Matter, that circle cannot be completed). Many Americans are taken back by that action. They cite disrespect for the military and police. But what about respect for all those who have been mistreated and killed needlessly? What about the disrespect for all those marginalized through inferiority and inequality in education, career opportunities, and healthcare? The flag represents them as well.

What happens when things get so bad in someone's life that the only thing they can think to do is to get down on their knees and pray? Seems like we as a country are at that point. So, when that national anthem plays, why not get down on both knees (or one if you prefer), bow your head, and ask for direction and forgiveness for our country? How powerful would that be!?

I don't know how many players and coaches in the NFL may take a knee this season. But more and more are speaking out.

Matt Ryan is one. He's the veteran, NFL MVP quarterback of the Atlanta Falcons. He's White. He's always pretty much led by example and is not necessarily known as a firebrand. Yes, he's worked quietly in the community with Children's Healthcare and the Boys & Girls Club of Metro Atlanta. Yet, after the killing of Floyd, Ryan made a $500 thousand contribution to help raise a total of $2 million for Atlanta's "Advancing the Lives of the Black Community." He began to become more vocal as well.

"I think the time has come," he said, "when silence isn't good enough."

That is why when athletes step to the podium with something to say, it's good to listen. For many, silence just isn't good enough anymore.

*I never understood the "shut up and play" mentality. That seemed almost plantation-esque. "You are here to do one thing. Perform for our enjoyment. You aren't allowed to think, have an opinion, nor share experiences from your past." We, ourselves, have opinions. Are we jealous because we don't have the stage to be heard by more than those*

around us? Or do some of us just not care about issues that impact society each and every day, so long as they don't mess up our lives. After all, we come first, right? I suspect it may be that we don't agree with the opinions being espoused. That's fine. We can't all agree. But it doesn't hurt to listen. Sometimes, we learn something by listening.

You can tell this is a topic near and dear to me. Having a career in the sports, television, and entertainment industry gets one close to the action and the players. Some players, you're right, I wouldn't give you two nickels for. But there are many who really, really want to make a difference and change things. Help the community. Help those less fortunate. Change the political climate. Share their faith. I continue to scratch my head when I hear a person denigrate an athlete for taking a knee to exemplify his grief for injustice and the least of those in society, while that critical person does a similar act in church or beside his bed albeit with, perhaps, a different tune in his head. The National Anthem ends "in the land of the free and the home of the brave." I can't help but hear that phrase and think of how Christ freed us from the slavery of sin and the incredible bravery he showed by dying on the cross. Take a stand. Take a knee. Be nailed to a cross. Make a difference.

# America's Pastime:
# A Loss of Innocence

**Baseball. America's pastime. While Ken Burns eloquently** tells the tale of baseball's lure and lore in his Emmy award-winning documentary series, I remember the game more like the movie *Summer of '42*—a gradual loss of innocence.

I was introduced to the game by my best friend. Jake was the youngest of three boys, so he was used to getting beat and beat up. That gave him incredible resolve and determination. As his best friend, and someone whom he could actually beat, he beat those traits into me as well. Jake ended up going to Princeton and became an acclaimed West Coast sportswriter. I learned a lot from him.

We lived in the country so, outside of Jake, there were precious few playmates. My older sister would have to do some days. She would lock me in my room and play teacher-student. Other days, I would drag her outside to pitch to me. She was a damn good pitcher and hitter. Not a bad teacher either.

The high school team was good. Very good. Four straight division and three straight league titles. I was good, too. Good enough to get a professional tryout before heading off to play baseball at a southern university.

But as much as I loved the game—and I did love it more than anything—I began to see some of life's dirty little secrets while boning my bat and oiling my glove. One summer our team made the playoffs and had to travel to the big city for a tournament. Our coach took the team to get lunch between games. We were told we had to leave.

"Him," said the establishment's manager, pointing to my dark-skinned teammate. So, we left.

That same coach often carted several of his players to away games in his station wagon. I enjoyed the camaraderie with my teammates. I didn't enjoy the stop at the local watering hole on the way back so Ol' Coach could throw back a few with his buds then attempt to drive us the rest of the way home.

College ball was a step up. Everyone was good. Northern colleges loved coming south early in the season. The weather was warmer, sans snow, and the coeds were prettier. We'd catch one of the mega universities on their way down to Florida and drill them. We thought we were pretty good. Then ten days later, on their way back after a dozen or so games in the Sunshine State, it was us who would get the drilling.

Competition within the team was fierce. If you got hurt, there was a good chance your job would not be there when you healed. So, you played hurt. Or tried. A pulled groin was one thing, but a separated shoulder, well, that's one you can't fake your way through.

You begin to ask yourself if those Yankee pinstripes will ever be a part of your future. When reality sets in and you understand that the answer is "No," what happens next?

After all those years, you sit there on the bench at what you know is going to be the last game you ever play and wonder how you've gone from professional prospect to bench warmer.

You've seen a lot. Experienced a lot. Most of all, you've probably learned a lot, like how to handle an unlevel and disruptive playing field and whatever else life might throw at you. All good lessons learned from America's pastime.

*Growing up is fun. We don't think so at the time. We all yearn to be "adults" so we can "do whatever we want." But it's not always easy. As our brains and emotions mature, we see and hear things that are, well, unsettling. Fairness. Unfairness. Racial bias. Outright racism. Advantages.*

*Inequities. All are part of the maturation process. I've always thought that sport was a great teacher. For me, it was baseball. The thrill of victory. The agony of defeat. The lessons learned weren't always pretty.*

# The Answer, My Friend

**Ever notice how what was once old is now new again** and what is new is, actually, really old? Like bell bottom pants and Nehru jackets. Okay. Bad examples.

What comes around, goes around? What goes around, comes around?

Are there really any new ideas anymore?

Well, of course there are. Technology and innovation change our landscape daily. Autonomous cars. Tik Tok. Artificial intelligence. Bitcoin. Cyber intelligence. Cyber security. mRNA vaccines.

We could go on and on.

What about music? Jazz. Blues. Bluesy Jazz. Reggae. Sca. Gospel. Hard rock. Southern Rock. Country. Country Rock. Rap. Christian Contemporary. Easy Listening. Opera. Classical. Classical Jazz. See, we've worked our way back to the beginning of the list.

But let's face it. No matter what your music preference, good lyrics are good lyrics.

Give me Bob Dylan.

"Positively Fourth Street." "Forever Young." "Knockin' on Heaven's Door." "The Times They Are A-Changin'." "Mr. Tambourine Man." "Like A Rollin' Stone."[30]

And of course, his greatest in my estimation—"Blowin' in the Wind".[31]

Written by him and Tom Petty in a matter of minutes, it was originally viewed as a protest song of that era. The era of bell bottom pants. And Nehru jackets.

But over the years, we have seen it deal with the universalities of life—many of which we wish we could escape.

It asks, *how many roads must a man walk down before you call him a man?* Good question. What must a man, a person, experience before he figures it all out? And contribute to society?

*How many times must the cannonballs fly before they're forever banned?* While cannonballs have transitioned to mortar fire, and bullets gun down innocent lives in America every single day, I often feel like this question is even more relevant today than when written in 1963. I think the answer to the question is never. Sadly.

*And how many years can some people exist, before they're allowed to be free?* Ask our Native Americans and Black brothers and sisters. I bet you would get an answer that would break your heart.

*And how many times can a man turn his head and pretend that he just doesn't see?* Every. Single. Day.

*And how many ears must one man have before he can hear people cry?* More than two. Regrettably.

*And how many deaths will it take 'til he knows, that too many people have died?* From war. AIDS. Cancer. Heart disease. COVID-19. Random killings. Curable maladies— scientific or social.

Dylan and Petty say the answer is blowin' in the wind. When I listen to the wind, I hear the voice of God.

Perhaps that's the answer.

*Who doesn't love music? Some have definite genres and artists they love. Others simply love it all. I am somewhere in between. I try at least to appreciate those sounds that don't resonate as well as others. I even try to pretend to like opera. About as close as I get is Andre Bocelli, admittedly one of my favorites. His rendition of "The Prayer" with Celine Dion is magical—and a bit operatic. My favorites, though, are those with lyrics that have a message. Give me a song that rips my heart out or inspires my social consciousness, and I'm all in. That's one reason why I like Dylan so much. His lyrics always seemed to nail it. "Blowin' in the Wind" expresses such easy, yet clear, thoughts. Now, I don't think that he and Tom Petty were anywhere near suggesting that the wind*

represented God. But I've also always believed that interpretation is often left to the listener and his heart. Which is why I enjoy love songs so much. Barry White? Bring it!

# Piano Man

**Nope. Not about Billy Joel. But I love many of Billy Joel's** lyrics. I wish I could write like that. But I can't. So, I read a lot. I've professed that more than once.

My reading has become a lot more purposeful. I think I only read one piece of fiction, John Grisham's, *The Guardian*, recently. I used to read a lot of Grisham.

Love his love for the game of baseball as much as his writings. Little known fact. His son played at the University of Virginia, and as the story goes, Grisham built the Cavaliers a new baseball stadium.

While fiction, *The Guardians* was a disturbing tale about imprisoned inmates who were innocent. The guardians, thankfully, were able to secure justice in the end.

Other recent reads and recommendations are in no particular order: *Shoe Dog* by Phil Knight, *Becoming* by Michelle Obama, *His Truth is Marching On* by Jon Meacham, *One* by Dennis Rouse, *White Like Me* by Tim Wise, *The Idealist* by George Hirthler, a re-read of *The Purpose Driven Life* by Rick Warren, *White Lies* by Daniel Hill and Pulitzer Prize winner Isabel Wilkerson's *Caste*.[32]

Another is Emmanuel Acho's *Uncomfortable Conversations with a Black Man*, named after his award-winning video series of the same name. Lots of insight. And yes, a bit uncomfortable at times. But it's supposed to be. Addressing systemic racism is not an easy topic.

I liked his description of the piano. Not uncomfortable at all. Rather inspiring, quite actually.

> "My favorite instrument to play is the piano. I taught myself how to play in college in breaks between training

camp practices when there wasn't enough time to nap. Turned out I loved it. During the most grueling parts of my time in the NFL, it kept me calm. Every day getting back from practice I would hop on my keyboard for a while. I still play even now. When I bought my first home in Austin, the first thing I purchased was a piano.

The beautiful thing about the piano is that you got white keys and you got black keys. And the only way to make the most beautiful, magnificent, and poetic noise is with both sets of keys working in tandem. You can't just play all the white keys, because you won't maximize what the instrument has to offer. You can't just play all the black keys, because you won't maximize what the instrument has to offer. But integrate the white and black keys together, and that is when the piano makes a joyful noise.

That's what this "we" is all about. If we can truly integrate white people and black people together, working in tandem, that's when our world will make a joyful noise."[33]

While I'm not sure all my reading will foster a joyful-noise stage career, I do believe I must learn to play those keys better.

*If you've discerned anything from reading Me, Jesus, a Beer, and a Cigar, it's my passion and focus on racial reconciliation. God made one race. He intended us to live in harmony. Sadly, we have failed. But we can get better. I believe much of the strife over the last several years has made us focus on how to do that better. Sure, we have a long way to go. And we can't get there without God. But those Black Keys and White Keys make the most incredible music when they play together.*

# ONE FINAL THOUGHT

# As Life Flickers Away

**He sat in front of the fireplace, a glass of wine in hand.**
It was a cold, winter's night. He could hear the wind and wolves howling outside.

He had retreated to his mountain home earlier in the day, before the winds and icy dusting arrived. He came alone. He needed time alone.

Age was setting in. For the wine, that was good. For him, it was not.

He understood that he was truly blessed. But as he looked into the fire and the recesses of his life, he wondered if it was good enough. Was it all good enough?

Good enough for what?

He knew that his faith and God's grace assured him a joy-filled, pain-free afterlife. He had peace in that assurance. It brought calm as the flames lightened much of the otherwise dark room.

Yet, he was bereft. So little time left. The window of his life was closing. He had caught incredible fire for God's love and understanding these last few years. Wisdom. Grace. Fellowship. Patience. Peace. Ministering to the least of these.

He was not retired. He did not want to retire. Or did he? Would it afford him more time? More time to do what? Love his wife? Love his friends? Love his family? Love strangers? He was certain that as cliché-ish as it might sound, love was the answer.

But where were the opportunities. He prayed. Ideas for new opportunities. Opportunities for new ideas. He had some. But he needed more? Why? Why did he need more?

"I just haven't done enough," he said as he prayed. "God gave me all these incredible gifts and talents and for so long, I squandered them. My faith is such a shallow faith without works. I need more works. I want more works. Works bring joy to my life."

So why was he so distraught as he sat in front of the fire? He knew his time was running out. He knew the disease would eventually take over. And shut the door. How much time did he have?

He prayed for patience. He prayed for peace. He prayed for understanding. He prayed for wisdom. He finally prayed for forgiveness for not allowing God to take complete control and play out the final scenes of his existence.

"There is so much I want to do for Him since I failed so miserably when I was younger."

God knows that. He has forgiven you. March to His flicker. Not yours.

*I debated whether I even wanted to put a commentary with my finale thought. And I really don't have much to add here. I'd simply like you, the reader, to read it more than once. And ask many of the same questions. No matter what age, I think you must ask yourself these questions. And come to understand. It is His path. And He will direct. If you just let Him. No matter how much or little time you have left.*

# Postlude

**I began this project wanting to provide "thoughts for** everyday living." But not just "everyday" thoughts. I admitted up front that many of the thoughts could have quite an edge to them. I'm certain there are many who have read the entries and felt I stepped over the line a bit. Or wouldn't have positioned a topic that way. Or was even wrong in the position I took. But that's what I hoped to accomplish. Contemplation. Thought.

Far too often, I've seen person after person, including me, live simply on the surface. And by that I mean, just wanting to skate by without ruffling any feathers so their life could be as comfortable as possible. But there are so many people in this world, particularly in American society, who don't have the privilege to skate by. The chips have been cast against them. And many of us don't notice or may not even care just so long as it doesn't impact our comfortable little lives. Please take time to notice.

Among the messages that I hope have been driven home in this book is don't be afraid to "get uncomfortable." Until one is prepared to do that, little progress is going to be made in society, in politics or in the church.

To risk being uncomfortable, one has to prepare mentally, spiritually and emotionally to act. In "Recognize, Decide, Do" I talk about the 16-year-old Black student from a challenged part of urban America and his mentor who very matter-of-factly laid it all out. Recognize the problem. Decide something needs to be done. And then do it. Don't wait for others. Take action. In "Ch-Ch-Ch-Ch-Changes," I confess to having a war with God wondering why he isn't giving me answers when I'm so willing to listen. He challenges me with "just do something." He'll let me know if it's the wrong path or not. We can sit around all our lives wondering what to do next or what God's plan is for us. I assure you, it isn't to do nothing. Or to wait forever for a revelation in the middle of the night.

I didn't hesitate to tackle difficult subjects like homelessness, rape, abortion, affluence, narrow-mindedness, racism, marriage, perspective and lack thereof, forgiveness, loneliness, hypocrisy, patriotism, death, grace and love.

Some of you will say, yes, but all from your perspective. I don't think so. Before I sat down to write *Me, Jesus, a Beer, and a Cigar*, I had a long chat with God. In that conversation, I said, "Lord, you've given me talents and gifts. Please show me how to use them, because I'm not sure I know how, and time's running out." I acknowledged that like Moses, I probably wasn't a great speaker or presenter—although I hope I'm getting better at that. And with each "thought," I did not begin writing without prayer and His guidance. Perhaps not as divinely inspired as The Bible—but inspired. As I re-read the everyday thoughts over and over again, there is not one in which I didn't feel the good Lord speaking through me.

Maybe I didn't dial it up perfectly. But there are perspectives that many, including and especially, professed Christians need to hear. I'm particularly hard on White evangelicals whose failure to admit unconscious bias and adherence to privilege, leads them down a disturbing path socially, racially and politically, not to mention spiritually.

There will be many of my friends who are surprised that I have tackled these topics and put a Christian twist to most all. But that is who I am. Yes, there are probably many who will say much like my friend did in "I Never Knew." But that is another reason why these thoughts are so important for me to share.

Not simply because I want people to think about everyday topics in ways they perhaps have never thought of them before, but to know what and who inspires me. If that has not always been apparent in my life, I plead guilty.

Finally, I hope there were entries that simply made you smile. We all need to smile. And many of us do it far too infrequently. "The

Hammer" about a baseball diamond cut in my backyard where heroes were made was a delightful memory from my childhood. A childhood that was happy and fulfilling in many ways. But lonely in others. One that certainly gave me plenty of time to develop my creativity. In the "Sunday Drive," I trust some of you had the chance to either re-live yesteryear or even pile into the car in current time and take that magical ride to nowhere. Perhaps some of you recall songs that I referenced—"Blowin in the Wind" and "He Ain't Heavy, He's My Brother"—and smiled, full of amazing memories from those times. While others just laughed at tunes from the past, for which they had no frame of reference at all—much like Neru jackets and bell bottom pants in "The Answer My Friend." And then there were my just-for-fun car and truck stories of "Mustang and Sally" and "My Green Truck" that brought back great thoughts of my youth. We all should take time to cling to those times and memories. To me, they are the ones I often relish the most. And smile.

I've tried to write *Me, Jesus, a Beer, and a Cigar* to encourage people of all avenues—Christian, Black, White, Non-Christian, Agnostics, Atheists, Young, Middle Age, "Mature"—to think about things they perhaps never gave much thought to—or think more deeply with yet another perspective that may begin to provide some clarity and inspiration to those moments we face every day.

# Acknowledgements

**As I alluded to early in the book, writing a book is an** arduous task. It cannot be accomplished without a lot of help and encouragement. When I first began writing a weekly blog, it never dawned on me that it could result in a book until one day that new friend in Dallas, Adrianne Watson, said she was working on her own book and that I should consider one, too. I encourage readers to keep their eyes open for Sister Watson's book, *The Demise of the American Evangelical and the Church's Role in Racism and White Supremacy.* In addition, I owe Adrianne a huge thanks for helping me find Anita Battista, an amazing editor and new friend.

I also want to acknowledge my new friend and photographer extraordinaire Mark Meadows whom I pressed into eleventh hour service in order to capture the scene of my inspiration on the back deck of Currahee Brewing Company in Alpharetta, GA and appreciate Currahee for allowing me to continue to occupy space on their turf week after week. And a special shout out to my friend Cass, a Currahee regular, who more than occasionally came by to see friends and befriended me as I chipped away at my inspiration.

Then there is Jake Curtis. I alluded to Jake as the San Francisco sportswriter in "America's Pastime: Loss of Innocence." Jake was my best friend growing up. He took this reclusive farm kid and turned me into a real competitor. Jake earned a Princeton degree and went on to become an acclaimed writer for the San Francisco Chronicle. He still lives in the Bay Area.

Two important ministries to me are the One Race Movement and Bridging the Gap. Both have become valuable parts of my life as I've dedicated more strongly to Christ's teachings, becoming an advocate and activist for reconciliation among the races.

And finally, there is family. You should be able to tell that family is important to me since I made "Family" the book's first section. There are multiple mentions of my sister, Betty Ann, whom I've always considered my life-long friend and who has always been there for me and with me. And then there is my one-and-only Alexandra, my daughter whom I love beyond comprehension and featured in "Love Story," "A Tradition Unlike Any Other," and "Ch-Ch-Ch-Ch-Changes." If one doesn't begin to understand the concept of unconditional love after being a parent, then they need to get a heart transplant. She is an amazing young woman who fought through a lot before finding happiness with her great husband, Alex, whom I love like a son.

But one always saves the best to last: my wife, Eve. She has taught me so much. In addition to being the smartest person I know, she is absolutely the best person I know. She keeps me grounded, is more patient with me than I deserve, and keeps loving me even during times when I'm fairly unlovable. Her care and concern for others is beyond my comprehension sometimes. I just know the good Lord is preparing a special place for her in heaven somewhere. She deserves that after dealing with me these many years and patiently guiding me through the many months to bring *Me, Jesus, a Beer, and a Cigar* to fruition. Her prayers, much like mine, hope that some of the inspired words will actually make a difference in someone's life, even if it's just one.

# Endnotes

1  Dickinson, Bob. "75 Scriptures to Guide Your Vote." *Like the Dew, A Progressive Journal of Southern Culture and Politics,* October 13, 2020.

2  Kahlil Gibran, "On Marriage," in *The Prophet* (New York: Alfred A. Knopf, 1923).

3  Landis, John. Director. 1978. *Animal House.* Universal Pictures.

4  Buffalo Springfield. "For What It's Worth." Dec. 13, 1966. Single. Atco Records, 1966; Barry Sadler, "Ballad of the Green Berets." 1966. Track 1 on *The Ballad of the Green Berets.* RCA, 1966

5  The Hollies. "He Ain't Heavy, He's My Brother." 1969 November. Track 16 on *Hollies Sing Hollies.* Parlophone, 1969

6  Math. 25: 45 (NIV)

7  Mishel, Lawrence and Wolfe, Julia. "CEO Compensation as Grown 940 Percent Since 1978." Economic Policy Institute, August 14, 2019.

8  "How much is given? By whom? For what?" CharityChoices.com, 2017

9  Sam Roberts,. "Minorities in U.S. Set to Become Majority by 2042." *New York Times.* August 14, 2008.

10  Patrick J. Buchanan, "The Emergency Existential Crisis at the Border." Syndicated column, March 10, 2021.

11  Col. 3:8; James 1:19 (NASB)

12  Ephesian 4: 25-26 (NASB)

13  Genesis 28: 10-22 (NASB)

14   *Dallas*. 1978-91. Season 9, episode 31. "Blast from the Past." directed by Michael Preece. aired May 16, 1986 on CBS; Zucker, Jerry. Director. 1990. *Ghost*. Paramount Pictures; *The Good Fight*. 2017-2021. Season 4, episode 1. "The Gang Deals with Alternate Reality." directed by Brooke Kennedy. aired April 9, 2020. CBS.

15   James 3 (NASB)

16   Richard Carlson Ph.D., *Don't Sweat the Small Stuff ... and it's all small stuff.* (Hatchette Books, 1997).

17   Rom. 1:29-31; 1 Peter 2:1 (NASB)

18   George Orwell, *1984*. (Secker & Warburg, 1949); William Golding, *The Lord of the Flies*. (Faber and Faber, 1954).

19   Andrew Romano and Dylan Stableford, "The Most Unusual Day: How March 11, 2020, Marked the Start of the Covid Era." *Yahoo News*, March 9, 2021

20   Frost, Robert. "The Road Not Taken." *Atlantic Monthly: A Group of Poems."* August, 1915.

21   Matt. 5: 1 – 7: 27(NASB)

22   Wikipedia. 2021. "The Shooting of Michael Brown." August 22, 201. https://en.wikipedia.org/wiki/Shooting_of_Michael_Brown

23   Oliver Milman, "Greenland's Melting Ice Raised Global Sea Level by 2.2mm in Two Months." *The Guardian*, March 19, 2020.

24   Tyler Carson, "Air Pollution Kills Far More People Than Covid Ever Will." *Bloomberg*. March 10, 2021; J.J Mai, "U.N. Warns Number of People Starving to Death Could Double Amid Pandemic." *National Public Radio, Mercy Corp.*, May 5, 2020; "20 Facts About Food Waste." *Earth.org*, July 19, 2021.

25   John Steinbeck, *East of Eden*. (The Viking Press, 1952).

26   Luke 22: 54-62 (NASB)

27   Isabel Wilkerson, *Caste-The Origins of Our Discontent*. (Penguin Random House, 2020). xv-xvii.

28  Rick Warren, *The Purpose Driven Life: What on Earth are We Here For.* (Zondervan, 2002); John Ortberg, *If You Want to Walk on Water, You Have to Get Out of the Boat.* (Zondervan, 2001).

29  Rev. Dr. Martin Luther King, Jr., *Why We Can't Wait* , (New American Library, 1963).

30  Bob Dylan. "Positively Fourth Street." 1965. Track 1 on *Positively Fourth Street*. Columbia. 1965; "Forever Young." 1973. Track 6 on *Planet Waves*. Asylum. 1974; "Knockin' on Heaven's Door." 1973. Track 7 on *Pat Garrett and Billy the Kid*. Columbia. 1973; "The Times They Are A'Changin'." 1963. Track 1 on *The Times They Are A'Changin'*. Columbia. 1964; "Mr. Tambourine Man." 1964. Track 8 on *Bringing It All Back Home*. Columbia. 1965; "Like a Rollin' Stone." 1965. Track 1 on *Highway 61 Revisited*. Columbia. 1965.

31  Bob Dylan. "Blowin' in the Wind." 1963. Track 1 on *The Freewheelin' Bob Dylan*. Columbia. 1963.

32  Phil Knight, *Shoe Dog*. (Scribner, 2018); Michelle Obama, *Becoming*. (Viking Press, 2018); Jon Meacham, *His Truth is Marching On – John Lewis and the Power of Hope* (Random House, 2020); Dennis Rouse, *One – Healing the Racial Divide*. (Avail, 2020); Tim Wise, *White Like Me*. (Soft Skull Press, 2007); George Hirthler, *The Idealist*. (Ringworks Press, 2017); Rick Warren, *The Purpose Driven Life*. (Zondervan, 2002); Isabel Wilkerson, *Caste*. Penguin Random House, 2020).

33  Emmanuel Acho, *Uncomfortable Conversations with a Black Man*. (Flatiron Books, EA Enterprises, LLC. 2020).

CPSIA information can be obtained
at www.ICGtesting.com
Printed in the USA
LVHW081511060322
712761LV00016B/949